S0-BOF-696

PLAINFIELD PUBLIC LIBRARY
15025 S. Illinois Street
Plainfield, IL 60544

WINTER
KNITTING

First published in the United Kingdom in 2014 by
Pavilion
1 Gower Street
London
WC1E 6HD

Copyright © Pavilion Books Company Ltd 2014
Text and pattern copyright © MillaMia 2014

All rights reserved. No part of this publication may be
copied, displayed, extracted, reproduced, utilised, stored
in a retrieval system or transmitted in any form or by
any means, electronic, mechanical or otherwise
including but not limited to photocopying, recording,
or scanning without the prior written permission of the
publishers. The patterns contained in this book and
the items created from them are for personal use only.
Commercial use of either the patterns or items made
from them is strictly prohibited.

ISBN 978-1-90939-790-3

A CIP catalogue record for this book is available from the
British Library.

10 9 8 7 6 5 4 3 2 1

Reproduction by Mission, Hong Kong
Printed and bound by Toppan Leefung Printing Ltd, China

This book can be ordered direct from the publisher at
www.pavilionbooks.com

WINTER

PATTERNS FOR THE FAMILY AND HOME KNITTING

MILLAMIA

SWEDEN

Photography by Emma Norén

PLAINFIELD PUBLIC LIBRARY
15025 S. Illinois Street
Plainfield, IL 60544

PAVILION

CONTENTS

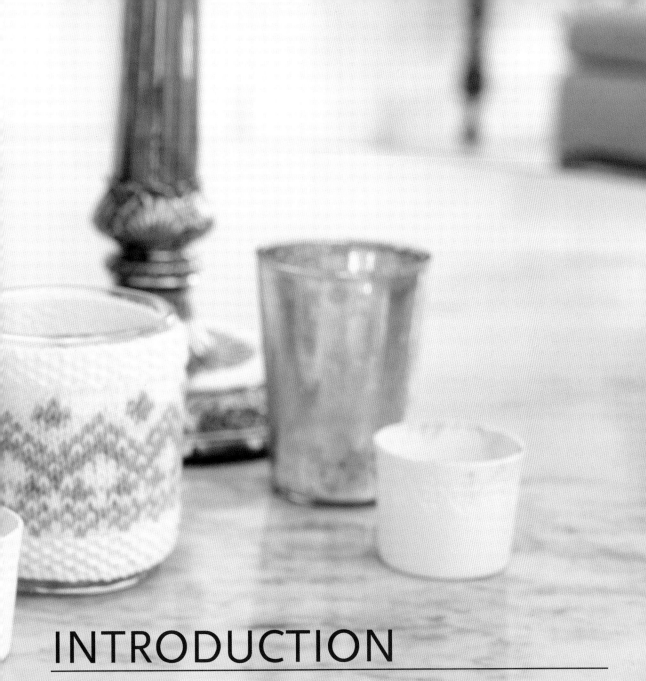

INTRODUCTION

When we think of winter in our homeland of Sweden there are some immediate associations that come to mind. As the seasons change from cool, crisp autumn to the cold and dark of winter, Scandinavians are particularly good at easing this transition with clothing, interiors and food that bring warmth and light. We wanted to share some of these wonderful traditions, designs and activities with you – but of course with the signature modern twist that we at MillaMia bring to all things knitted.

In this book you will find a mix of knitting projects to see you through the winter season. Indulge in kitting yourself out for the first fall of snow, make clothes that the kids can wear for the festive season and create interior projects that will bring warmth both literally and visually. You will also find that we have added a couple of 'bonus' projects – sharing a couple of our favourite festive recipes along with some wonderful paper projects that are perfect for any yarn enthusiast.

BEFORE YOU START

SKILL LEVELS

Recognising that we are not all expert knitters, we have graded each pattern in the book to allow you to gauge whether it is one that you feel confident to try.

SOME ADVICE

As there can be colour variations between dye lots when yarn is produced, we suggest that you buy all the yarn required for a project at the same time (with the same dye lot number) to ensure consistency of colour. The amount of yarn required for each pattern is based on average requirements, meaning the quantities given are an approximate guide.

The designs in this book have been created specifically with a certain yarn composition in mind. The weight, quality, colours, comfort and finished knit effect of this yarn are ideally suited to these patterns. Substituting for another yarn may produce a garment that is different from the design and images in this book.

TENSION / GAUGE

A standard tension is given for all the patterns in this book. As the patterns are in different stitch types (e.g. stocking, garter, rib, etc) this tension may vary between patterns, and so you must check your tension against the recommendation at the start of the pattern. As matching the tension affects the final shape and size of the item you are knitting, it can have a significant impact if it is not matched. Ensuring that you are knitting to the correct tension will result in the beautiful shape and lines of the original designs being achieved.

To check your tension we suggest that you knit a square according to the tension note at the start of each pattern (casting on an additional 10 or more stitches to the figure given in the tension note and knitting 5 to 10 more rows than specified in the tension note). You should knit the tension square in the stitch given in the note (e.g. stocking, garter, moss, etc). Once knitted, mark out a 10cm/4in square using pins and count the number of stitches and rows contained within. If your tension does not quite match the one given, try switching to either finer needles (if you have too few stitches in your square) or thicker needles (if you have too many stitches) until you reach the desired tension.

USEFUL RESOURCES

We believe that using quality trims with our knitwear gives the garments a professional finishing touch. Visit your local yarn/haberdashery shop for these items and MillaMia yarn, or visit www.millamia.com to order yarn directly or find local stockists.

SIZES

Alongside the patterns in this book we give measurements for the items – as two children of the same age can have very different measurements, this should be used as a guide when choosing which size to knit. The best way to ensure a good fit is to compare the actual garment measurements given in the pattern with the measurements of an existing garment that fits the child well.

Please note that where a chest measurement is given in the table at the top of each pattern, this refers to the total measurement of the garment around the chest. When the cross chest measurement is given graphically in the accompanying diagrams, this is half the around chest measurement. Children's clothes are designed with plenty of 'ease', which means that there is not as much shaping or fit to a child's garment as you will find in adult knitwear.

CARE OF YOUR GARMENT

See the ball band of MillaMia Naturally Soft Merino for washing and pressing instructions. Make sure you reshape your garments while they are wet after washing, and dry flat.

LANGUAGE

This book has been written in UK English. However, where possible US terminology has also been included and we have provided a translation of the most common knitting terms that differ between UK and US knitting conventions on page 11. In addition all sizes and measurements are given in both centimetres and inches throughout. Remember that when a knitting pattern refers to the left and right sides of an item it is referring to the left or right side as worn, rather than as you are looking at it.

READING COLOUR CHARTS

For some of the patterns in this book there are colour charts included. In a colour chart one square represents one stitch and one row. A key shows what each colour in the chart refers to. The bottom row of the chart indicates the first row of knitting, and as you work your way up, each row of the chart illustrates the next row of knitting. Repeats are the same for all sizes, although different sizes will often require extra stitches as the repeat will not exactly fit. These stitches are marked by vertical lines showing the start and end of rows.

Additional specific instructions are given regarding how to read each chart in the 'Note' at the start of each pattern.

WHERE CAN I LEARN MORE?

We hope to make knitting easy for you. If there is a new technique you are struggling with or if you are a complete novice, there are some marvellous resources available to you. The internet is a wonderful thing – so many links and videos and tutorials at your fingertips, just a search away. If you need a starting point, log on to www.millamia.com and look through the 'Making Knitting Easy' section. There you can get advice, or download tools, email us a question for our technical experts, organise a knitting class or find someone who can help knit the item for you. Don't forget to look locally too. You should seek out any yarn shops or haberdashery departments. Many of these are staffed with real experts who will be able to help you. A full list of MillaMia stockists is available from our website www.millamia.com – in these stores you will find people who are familiar and experienced with both the MillaMia yarns and patterns.

TECHNIQUES

Some of you may not be familiar with Swiss darning, which is a technique we use on a few of the projects in this book. Please see the special instructions we have included on page 156 if you want some more help with this technique.

CONFUSED WITH A PATTERN?

We check every MillaMia pattern numerous times before we go to print. Despite this, occasionally there can be errors in knitting patterns. If you see what you think is an error, the best thing is to visit www.millamia.com where any errors that have been spotted will be published under 'Pattern Revisions'. If you cannot find the answer you are looking for, then do send an email (info@millamia.com) or contact us via the website and we will get back to you.

ABBREVIATIONS

alt	alternate
approx	approximately
beg	begin(ning)
cont	continue
dec	decrease(ing)
foll(s)	follow(s)(ing)
g-st	garter stitch
inc	increase(ing)
k or K	knit
k2 tog	knit two stitches together
k3 tog	knit three stitches together
m1	make one stitch by picking up the loop lying before the next stitch and knitting into back of it
m1p	make one stitch by picking up the loop lying before the next stitch and purling into back of it
p or P	purl
p2 tog	purl two stitches together
patt	pattern
pm	place marker
psso	pass slipped stitch over
pwise	purlwise
rib2 tog	rib two stitches together according to rib pattern being followed
rem	remain(ing)
rep	repeat(s)(ing)
rnd(s)	round(s)

skpo	slip one, knit one, pass slipped stitch over – one stitch decreased
s2kpo	slip two stitches as if to k2 tog, then pass two slipped stitches over – two stitches decreased
sl	slip stitch
sm	slip marker
ssk	slip two stitches one at a time as if to knit, put left needle into front of both stitches and knit together – one stitch decreased
st(s)	stitch(es)
st st	stocking stitch
tbl	through back of loop
tog	together
yf	yarn forward
yo	yarn over
yon	yarn over needle to make a stitch
yrn	yarn round needle
y2rn	wrap the yarn two times around needle. On the following row work into each loop separately, working tbl into second loop
[]	work instructions within brackets as many times as directed

UK AND US KNITTING TRANSLATIONS

UK	US
Cast off	Bind off
Colour	Color
Grey	Gray
Join	Sew
Moss stitch	Seed stitch
Stocking stitch	Stockinette stitch
Tension	Gauge
Yarn forward	Yarn over
Yarn over needle	Yarn over
Yarn round needle	Yarn over
y2rn	yo2

KNITTING NEEDLE CONVERSION CHART

Metric (mm)	US size
2.75	2
3	2
3.25	3
3.75	5
5	8

WARMTH

THERE IS NOTHING LIKE KNITS MADE FROM
THE FINEST MERINO WOOL TO KEEP YOU WARM
ON COLD DAYS AND NIGHTS, OR SNUG AT HOME.

HONEY HONEY CUSHION

SKILL LEVEL BEGINNER / IMPROVING

SIZES / MEASUREMENTS

34cm/13$\frac{1}{2}$in by 34cm/13$\frac{1}{2}$in to fit a 35cm/13$\frac{3}{4}$in by 35cm/13$\frac{3}{4}$in cushion pad.

MATERIALS

Four 50g/1$\frac{3}{4}$oz balls of MillaMia Naturally Soft Merino in Putty Grey (121).
Pair of 3.25mm (US 3) knitting needles.
Cable needle.
5 buttons approx 19mm/$\frac{3}{4}$in in diameter.

TENSION / GAUGE

25 sts and 34 rows to 10cm/4in square over st st using
3.25mm (US 3) needles.

HINTS AND TIPS

This is a relaxing fun knit for any knitter to treat themselves with.
The cushion looks superb piled high on your bed or sofa – why not
knit a selection in toning colours to soften your interior look? With
a different construction on the front and back, the pattern is a very
manageable size and an excellent project for someone wanting to
master this waffle-like cable texture.

ABBREVIATIONS

C4F, cable 4 front – slip next 2 sts onto cable needle and hold at front of
work, k2, then k2 from cable needle.
C4B, cable 4 back – slip next 2 sts onto cable needle and hold at back
of work, k2, then k2 from cable needle.
See also page 11.

ALTERNATIVE COLOURWAYS

| Berry | Snow | Fawn | Sable | Plum |
| 163 | 124 | 160 | 105 | 162 |

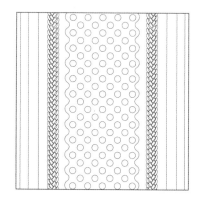

34 cm / 13½ in

34 cm / 13½ in

FRONT

With 3.25mm (US 3) needles cast on 86 sts.

1st row K5, p4, k4, p3, k8, p3, k32, p3, k8, p3, k4, p4, k5.

Inc row P18, m1, p4, m1, p7, [m1, p4] 7 times, m1, p7, m1, p4, m1, p18. 98 sts.

Cont in cable and rib patt.

1st row K5, p4, k4, p3, k2, [C4F] twice, p3, [C4B, C4F] 5 times, p3, k2, [C4F] twice, p3, k4, p4, k5.

2nd row P to end.

3rd row K5, p4, k4, p3, [C4B] twice, k2, p3, k40, p3, [C4B] twice, k2, p3, k4, p4, k5.

4th row P to end.

5th row K5, p4, k4, p3, k2, [C4F] twice, p3, [C4F, C4B] 5 times, p3, k2, [C4F] twice, p3, k4, p4, k5.

6th row P to end.

7th row K5, p4, k4, p3, [C4B] twice, k2, p3, k40, p3, [C4B] twice, k2, p3, k4, p4, k5.

8th row P to end.

These 8 rows set the cable and rib patt.

Cont in patt until work measures 34cm/13$\frac{1}{2}$in from cast on edge, ending with a right side row.

Dec row P18, p2 tog, p2, p2 tog, p6, [p2 tog, p3] 7 times, p2 tog, p7, p2 tog, p2, p2 tog, p18. 86 sts.

Cast off.

BACK

Lower back

With 3.25mm (US 3) needles cast on 86 sts.

1st row K5, p4, k4, p3, k8, p3, k32, p3, k8, p3, k4, p4, k5.

2nd row P to end.

These 2 rows set the rib patt.

Cont in patt until back measures 27cm/10$\frac{1}{2}$in from cast on edge, ending with a p row.

Cast off in rib.

Upper back

With 3.25mm (US 3) needles cast on 86 sts.

1st row K5, p4, k4, p3, k8, p3, k32, p3, k8, p3, k4, p4, k5.

2nd row P to end.

These 2 rows set the rib patt.

Work a further 4 rows.

1st buttonhole row K5, [k2 tog, y2rn, skpo, patt 14] 4 times, k2 tog, y2rn, skpo, k5.

2nd buttonhole row P to end, working twice in y2rn.

Cont in patt until work measures 15cm/6in from cast on edge, ending with a p row.

Cast off in rib.

TO MAKE UP

Lap upper back over lower back for approx 8cm/3in and tack in place. With right sides together, sew back to front. Turn to right side. Sew on buttons. Insert cushion pad.

A SIMPLE BACK

HAVE FUN CHOOSING YOUR BUTTONS TO TONE OR TO CLASH.

SNOW STORM COWL

SKILL LEVEL BEGINNER / IMPROVING

SIZES / MEASUREMENTS

One size measuring 64cm/25¼in around by
22cm/8¾in high.

MATERIALS

Four 50g/1¾oz balls of MillaMia Naturally Soft
Merino in Forget me not (120) (M).
One ball of Snow (124) (C).
Pair of 3.25mm (US 3) knitting needles.

TENSION / GAUGE

25 sts and 34 rows to 10cm/4in square over st st
using 3.25mm (US 3) needles.

ALTERNATIVE COLOURWAYS

Storm
102

Snow
124

Berry
163

Snow
124

Pitch
Black
100

Snow
124

Storm
102

Lilac
Blossom
123

32 cm / 12½ in

22 cm / 8¾ in

HINTS AND TIPS

As with all Fair Isle patterns the trick is to not pull the yarn you are stranding behind the work too tight. This cowl can also be knitted in the round – see alternative instructions below.

ABBREVIATIONS

See page 11.

NOTE

When working from Chart, k rows are read from right to left and p rows from left to right. If worked in the round, all rnds are knit rnds and chart is always read from right to left.

COWL

With 3.25mm (US 3) needles and M cast on 162 sts.
Beg with a k row, work 40 rows in st st.
Cont in patt from Chart. Light colour is C, dark colour is M.
1st row Patt last st of Chart, [work across 16 st patt rep] 10 times, patt first st of Chart.
2nd row Patt last st of Chart, [work across 16 st patt rep] 10 times, patt first st of Chart.
These 2 rows set the Chart.
Cont in patt to end of row 70.
Cont in M only.
Work 40 rows st st.
Cast off.

TO MAKE UP

Join cast on edge to cast off edge. Turn cowl to right side. Using mattress stitch join ends together to form a circle.

COWL –KNIT IN THE ROUND VERSION

With 3.25mm (US 3) needles and M cast on 160 sts.
Work 40 rnds in st st.
Cont in patt from Chart. Light colour is C, dark colour is M.
1st rnd [Work across 16 st patt rep] 10 times.
2nd rnd [Work across 16 st patt rep] 10 times.
These 2 rnds set the Chart.
Cont in patt to end of rnd 70.
Cont in M only.
Work 40 rnds st st.
Cast off.

TO MAKE UP

Join cast on edge to cast off edge.

KEY

☐ M – Forget me not (120)
☐ C – Snow (124)

16 st rep

SNOW STORM
WRISTWARMERS

SKILL LEVEL BEGINNER / IMPROVING

SNOW STORM WRISTWARMERS

SKILL LEVEL BEGINNER / IMPROVING

SIZE
One size to fit adult woman.

MATERIALS
One 50g/1³/₄oz ball of MillaMia Naturally Soft Merino in each of Forget Me Not (120) (M) and Snow (124) (C).
Pair of 3.25mm (US 3) knitting needles.

TENSION / GAUGE
25 sts and 34 rows to 10cm/4in square over st st using 3.25mm (US 3) needles.

HINTS AND TIPS
A nice quick knit, these wristwarmers would make a fantastic gift. As with all Fair Isle projects, remember not to pull the yarn you are carrying on the back of the work too tight as this will cause the fabric to pucker.

ABBREVIATIONS
See page 11.

NOTE
When working from Chart, k rows are read from right to left and p rows from left to right.

ALTERNATIVE COLOURWAYS

Storm 102 Snow 124   Berry 163 Storm 102   Midnight 101 Putty Grey 121

9.5 cm / 3¾ in

26.5 cm / 10½ in

WRISTWARMERS

With 3.25mm (US 3) needles and M cast on 50 sts.
1st rib row K2, [p2, k2] to end.
2nd rib row P2, [k2, p2] to end.
These 2 rows form the rib.
Work a further 6 rows.
Beg with a k row, work in patt from Chart. Light colour is C, dark colour is M.
1st row Patt last st of Chart, [work across 16 st patt rep] 3 times, patt first st of Chart.
2nd row Patt last st of Chart, [work across 16 st patt rep] 3 times, patt first st of Chart.
These 2 rows set the Chart.
Cont in patt to end of row 70.
Cont in M only.
Work 8 rows rib.
Cast off in rib.

TO MAKE UP

Join side seams leaving a gap for thumb.

KEY

M – Forget me not (120)
C – Snow (124)

16 st rep

ARCTIC CUSHION

SKILL LEVEL IMPROVING

MEASUREMENTS

34cm/13½in by 34cm/13½in to fit a 35cm/13¾in by 35cm/13¾in cushion pad.

MATERIALS

Three 50g/1¾oz balls of MillaMia Naturally Soft Merino in Forget me not (120) (M).
One ball of Snow (124) (C).
Pair of 3.25mm (US 3) knitting needles.

TENSION / GAUGE

25 sts and 34 rows to 10cm/4in square over st st using 3.25mm (US 3) needles.

HINTS AND TIPS

This is a great way to try a Fair Isle pattern if you have not tried this style of knitting before. As a cushion has no shaping you can concentrate on the pattern alone. Also the back is much simpler! As with all Fair Isle knitting the trick is to not pull the yarn you are stranding too tightly across the back.

ABBREVIATIONS

See page 11.

NOTE

When working from Chart, k rows are right side rows and read from right to left, p rows are wrong side rows and read from left to right.

ALTERNATIVE COLOURWAYS

Midnight Snow
101   124

Pitch   Berry
Black   163
100

Snow   Scarlet
124   140

Midnight Fuchsia
101   143

34 cm / 13½ in

34 cm / 13½ in

FRONT

With 3.25mm (US 3) needles and M cast on 86 sts.
Beg with a k row, cont in st st.

1st row Using M, k to end.

2nd row Using C, p to end.

3rd row Using C, k to end.

Work in patt from Chart 1.

4th row P1M, [work across 1st row of 6 st patt rep]
14 times, p1M.

5th row K1M, [work across 2nd row of 6 st patt rep]
14 times, k1M.

These 2 rows set the Chart.

6th to 8th rows Work in patt to end of Chart.

9th row Using M, k to end.

10th row Using M, p to end, dec one st at centre of
last row. 85 sts.

Work in patt from Chart 2.

11th row Patt one st before patt rep, [work across 1st
row of 42 st patt rep] twice.

12th row [Work across 2nd row of 42 st patt rep]
twice, patt one st after patt rep.

These 2 rows set the Chart.

13th to 19th rows Work in patt to end of Chart.

20th row Using M, p to end.

21st row Using M, k to end, inc one st at centre of
last row. 86 sts.

Work in patt from Chart 3.

22nd row P1M, [work across 1st row of 6 st patt rep]
14 times, p1M.

23rd row K1M, [work across 2nd row of 6 st patt rep]
14 times, k1M.

These 2 rows set the Chart.

24th to 26th rows Work in patt to end of Chart.

27th row Using C, k to end.

28th row Using C, p to end, dec one st at centre of
last row. 85 sts.

Work in patt from Chart 4.

29th row Patt one st before patt rep, [work across 1st
row of 12 st patt rep] 7 times.

30th row [Work across 2nd row of 12 st patt rep] 7 times,
patt one st after patt rep.

These 2 rows set the Chart.

31st to 45th rows Work in patt to end of Chart.

Rep the 2nd to 45th rows once more, and then the
2nd to 27th rows again.

Next row Using C, p to end.

Next row Using M, k to end.

Cast off.

STRIPED BACK

With 3.25mm (US 3) needles and M cast on 85 sts.
Beg with a k row, cont in st st and stripes of 26 rows
M, 2 rows C, 17 rows M, 2 rows C, 23 rows M, 2 rows
C, 17 rows M, 2 rows C, 26 rows M.
Cast off.

TO MAKE UP

With right sides together, sew back to front along
3 sides. Turn to right side. Insert cushion pad. Join
remaining seam.

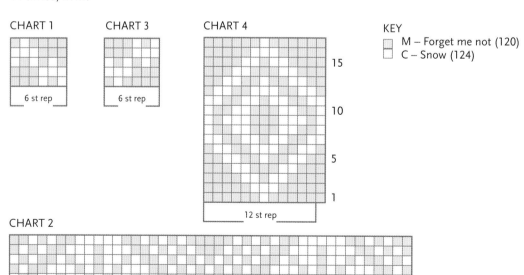

CHART 1

6 st rep

CHART 3

6 st rep

CHART 4

15

10

5

1

12 st rep

CHART 2

42 st rep

KEY

☐ M – Forget me not (120)

☐ C – Snow (124)

STRIPES, STRIPES, STRIPES

WE LOVE THE SIMPLE ELEGANCE OF THE BACK ON THIS DESIGN.

LYS CANDLE HOLDER

SKILL LEVEL BEGINNER (STRIPE VERSION);
BEGINNER / IMPROVING (FAIR ISLE VERSION)

SIZES / MEASUREMENTS
One size to fit a candle holder 8cm/3in high with 25cm/10in circumference.

MATERIALS
Fair Isle version
One 50g/1³/₄oz ball of MillaMia Naturally Soft Merino in each of Forget me not (120) (M) and Snow (124) (C).
Stripe version
One 50g/1³/₄oz ball of MillaMia Naturally Soft Merino in each of Forget me not (120) (M) and Storm (102) (C).
Both versions
Pair each of 3mm (US 2) and 3.25mm (US 3) knitting needles.

TENSION / GAUGE
25 sts and 34 rows to 10cm/4in square over st st using 3.25mm (US 3) needles.

HINTS AND TIPS
The Stripe version is a really quick, simple knit, perfect for the beginner who does not want to knit yet another garter stitch scarf. The Fair Isle version is actually a great way to try Fair Isle for the first time as it is a manageable size with no shaping, but just remember not to pull too tight when stranding the yarn along the back of the work.

ABBREVIATIONS
See page 11.

NOTE
When working from Chart, k rows are read from right to left and p rows from left to right.

12.5 cm / 5 in

8 cm / 3 in

ALTERNATIVE COLOURWAYS

Scarlet Snow
140   124

Storm Lilac
102   Blossom
       123

Midnight Snow
101   124

SOMETHING FOR THE BEGINNER

AN EASIER VERSION IN STRIPES – AND YOU CAN CHOOSE THE
COLOURS TO MATCH YOUR HOME.

FAIR ISLE VERSION

With 3mm (US 2) needles and C cast on 66 sts.
1st moss st row [K1, p1] to end.
2nd moss st row [P1, k1] to end.
Rep the last 2 rows twice more.
Change to 3.25mm (US 3) needles.
Beg with a k row, work in patt from Chart. Light colour
is C, dark colour is M.
1st row Patt last st of Chart, [work across 8 st patt rep]
8 times, patt first st of Chart.
2nd row Patt last st of Chart, [work across 8 st patt rep]
8 times, patt first st of Chart.
These 2 rows set the Chart.
Cont in patt to end of row 18.
Cont in C only.
Change to 3mm (US 2) needles.
Work 5 rows moss st.
Cast off in moss st.

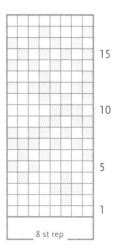

8 st rep

KEY
M – Forget me not (120)
C – Snow (124)

TO MAKE UP

Join side seams.

STRIPE VERSION

With 3mm (US 2) needles and M cast on 66 sts.
1st moss st row [K1, p1] to end.
2nd moss st row [P1, k1] to end.
Rep the last 2 rows twice more.
Change to 3.25mm (US 3) needles.
Beg with a k row, work in st st and stripes of [2 rows M,
2 rows C] 4 times, 2 rows M.
Cont in M only.
Change to 3mm (US 2) needles.
Work 5 rows moss st.
Cast off in moss st.

TO MAKE UP

Join side seams.

STICKA CARDS

TENSION SQUARES – THE BANE OF ANY KNITTER'S LIFE! WE ALL KNOW WE ARE SUPPOSED TO DO THEM, BUT SO FEW OF US ACTUALLY HAVE THE DISCIPLINE TO SIT DOWN AND CAST ON FOR THAT SMALL SQUARE THAT WILL HELP MAKE THE DIFFERENCE AND ENSURE THAT THE END RESULT OF OUR KNITTING ACTUALLY MEASURES UP AS IT SHOULD. WE WERE THRILLED THEREFORE WHEN KIRSTEN IN OUR TEAM CAME UP WITH THIS FABULOUS IDEA FOR HOW WE COULD PUT TENSION SQUARES TO GREAT USE. WHY NOT MAKE AMAZING GREETING CARDS, SHE SUGGESTED? WE LOVED THIS IDEA AND HELENA AND YUMIKO, OUR INTERN AT THE TIME, SPENT AFTERNOONS COMING UP WITH WONDERFUL, SIMPLE YET EFFECTIVE CUTOUT IDEAS FOR THESE CARDS. DID YOU KNOW 'STICKA' MEANS 'TO KNIT' IN SWEDISH?

STICKA CARDS

SIZES / MEASUREMENTS
Makes a 15cm/6in square greeting card.

MATERIALS (PER CARD)
One 10cm/4in square tension swatch.
45cm/18in by 15cm/6in rectangle of card in your choice of colour.
Scalpel / sharp knife.
Cutting board.
Glue or tape.

TO MAKE

1 If your card is not already the right size, cut out a 45cm/18in by 15cm/6in rectangle. Starting at the left hand side, measure 15cm/6in and 30cm/12in along the long edges of the rectangle. Score vertically on the wrong side at these points to divide the card into three sections.

2 Draw the pattern you want to cut out onto the centre section on the wrong side of the card, then cut out using a scalpel or sharp knife. Visit www.millamia.com to download templates for the cut-out motifs.

3 Place the tension square in the centre of the card behind the cutout pattern and secure in place with some glue or tape – remember to put the right side of the fabric so that it shows through the opening.

4 Fold the right hand section of the card over the wrong side of the cutout section, dabbing some glue on the wrong side to secure in place. Complete the card by folding along the remaining scored line. Allow the glue to dry before using.

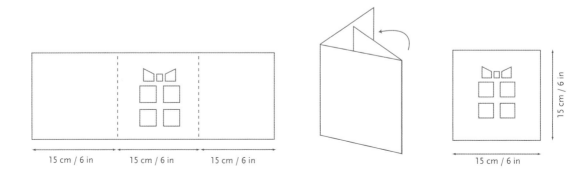

15 cm / 6 in   15 cm / 6 in   15 cm / 6 in   15 cm / 6 in

15 cm / 6 in

COLOUR

WHO SAYS HAND KNITS HAVE TO BE MUTED AND TRADITIONAL?
WE LOVE TO PLAY WITH COLOUR – COLOURS THAT CLASH AND
FIRE OFF EACH OTHER BRING THESE PIECES TO LIFE.

JOSEPH TANK TOP

SKILL LEVEL BEGINNER

SIZES / MEASUREMENTS

To fit age	1–2	3–4	5–6	7–8	years

ACTUAL MEASUREMENTS

Chest	52	56	61	66	cm
	20½	22	24	26	in
Length to shoulder	30	34	39	45	cm
	12	13½	15½	17¾	in

MATERIALS

2(2:3:3) 50g/1¾oz balls of MillaMia Naturally Soft Merino in Midnight (101) (M).
One ball in each of Scarlet (140) (A) and Peacock (144) (B).
Pair each of 3mm (US 2) and 3.25mm (US 3) knitting needles.

TENSION / GAUGE

25 sts and 34 rows to 10cm/4in square over st st using 3.25mm (US 3) needles.

HINTS AND TIPS

A great beginner knit, this is a simple yet effective piece that will liven up any boy's outfit. It is easy to cast off too tight, which can cause problems if the child you are knitting for has a larger head. A tip therefore is to consider using a larger knitting needle when casting off the neckband for a looser result.

ABBREVIATIONS

See page 11.

26 (28 : 30.5 : 33) cm
10¼ (11 : 12 : 13) in

30 (34 : 39 : 45) cm
12 (13½ : 15½ : 17¾) in

ALTERNATIVE COLOURWAYS

Forget me not 120   Snow 124   Fawn 160   Seaside 161   Plum 162   Claret 104

BACK

With 3mm (US 2) needles and A cast on 66(70:78:82) sts.
1st rib row K2, [p2, k2] to end.
2nd rib row P2, [k2, p2] to end.
Rep the last 2 rows 3(4:4:5) times more, inc 1(3:1:3) sts evenly across last row. 67(73:79:85) sts.
Change to 3.25mm (US 3) needles and M.
Beg with a k row, cont in st st until back measures 18(21:25:30)cm/
7(8¼:10:12)in from cast on edge, ending with a p row.
Shape armholes
Cast off 5 sts at beg of next 2 rows. 57(63:69:75) sts **.
Next row K2, skpo, k to last 4 sts, k2 tog, k2.
Next row P to end.
Rep the last 2 rows 4(5:6:7) times more. 47(51:55:59) sts.
Cont in st st until back measures 30(34:39:45)cm/12(13½:15½:17¾)in from cast on edge, ending with a p row.
Shape shoulders
Cast off 9(10:11:12) sts at beg of next 2 rows. 29(31:33:35) sts.
Cast off.

FRONT

Work as given for back to **.
Shape front neck
Next row K2, skpo, k21(24:27:30), k2 tog, k1, turn and work on these sts for first side of front neck.
Next row P to end.
Next row K2, skpo, k to last 3 sts, k2 tog, k1.
Next row P to end.
Rep the last 2 rows 3(4:5:6) times more. 18(19:20:21) sts.
Keeping armhole edge straight, cont to dec at neck edge on 6 foll alt rows then every foll 4th row until 9(10:11:12) sts rem.
Cont straight until front measures same as back to shoulder, ending at armhole edge.
Shape shoulder
Cast off.
With right side facing, slip centre st onto a safety pin, join on yarn to rem sts, k1, skpo, k to last 4 sts, k2 tog, k2.
Next row P to end.
Next row K1, skpo, k to last 4 sts, k2 tog, k2.
Next row P to end.
Rep the last 2 rows 3(4:5:6) times more. 18(19:20:21) sts.
Keeping armhole edge straight, cont to dec at neck edge on 4 foll alt rows then every foll 4th row until 9(10:11:12) sts rem.
Cont straight until front measures same as back to shoulder, ending at armhole edge.
Shape shoulder
Cast off.

NECKBAND

Join right shoulder seam.

With right side facing, using 3mm (US 2) needles and A, pick up and k38(42:44:48) sts evenly down left side of front neck, k1 from safety pin, pick up and k38(40:44:46) sts evenly up right side of front neck, 32(34:36:38) sts from back neck. 109(117:125:133) sts.

3rd and 4th sizes only

1st row [P2, k2] –(–:20:21) times, p1, [k2, p2] to end.

1st and 2nd sizes only

1st row [K2, p2] 17(18:–:–) times, k2, p1, k2, [p2, k2] to end.

All sizes

This row sets the rib.

2nd row Rib 37(41:43:47), s2kpo, rib to end.

3rd row Rib to end.

4th row Rib 36(40:42:46), s2kpo, rib to end.

5th row Rib to end.

2nd, 3rd and 4th sizes only

6th row Rib –(39:41:45), s2kpo, rib to end.

7th row Rib to end.

3rd and 4th sizes only

8th row Rib –(–:40:44), s2kpo, rib to end.

9th row Rib to end.

All sizes

Cast off in rib, dec on this row as before.

Join left shoulder seam and neckband.

ARMBANDS

With right side facing, using 3mm (US 2) needles and B, pick up and k86(94:98:102) sts evenly around armhole edge.

1st row P2, [k2, p2] to end.

2nd row K2, [p2, k2] to end.

These 2 rows form the rib.

Work a further 5(7:7:9) rows.

Cast off in rib.

TO MAKE UP

Join side and armband seams.

POWER DRESSING

MAKE A STATEMENT WITH BOLD COLOUR CHOICES.

EVA DRESS

SKILL LEVEL BEGINNER / IMPROVING

SIZES / MEASUREMENTS

To fit age	1–2	2–3	3–4	4–5	5–6	6–7	years

ACTUAL MEASUREMENTS

Chest	51	56	61	65	70	75	cm
	20	22	24	25½	27½	29½	in

Length to back neck	45	50	55	60	65	70	cm
	17¾	19¾	21¾	23¾	25½	27½	in

Sleeve length	21	24	26	28	31	34	cm
	8¼	9½	10¼	11	12¼	13½	in

MATERIALS

3(3:4:4:5:5) 50g/1¾ oz balls of MillaMia Naturally Soft Merino in
Fuchsia (143) (M).
2(2:2:3:3:3) balls in each of Midnight (101) (A) and Daisy Yellow (142) (B).
Pair each of 3mm (US 2) and 3.25mm (US 3) knitting needles.
Circular 3.25mm (US 3) knitting needle.
4 buttons approx 12mm/½in in diameter.

TENSION / GAUGE

25 sts and 34 rows to 10cm/4in square over st st using
3.25mm (US 3) needles.

HINTS AND TIPS

Block the rib on the hem nice and wide to
achieve a sleek straight look to this dress.
Choosing strong colour combinations
ensures the desired visual colour block
effect is achieved.

ABBREVIATIONS

See page 11.

ALTERNATIVE COLOURWAYS

Storm
102   Snow
124   Scarlet
140   Petal
122   Putty
Grey
121   Storm
102

25.5 (28 : 30.5 : 32.5 : 35 : 37.5) cm
10 (11 : 12 : 12¾ : 13¾ : 14¾) in

21 (24 : 26 : 28 : 31 : 34) cm
8¼ (9½ : 10¼ : 11 : 12¼ : 13½) in

45 (50 : 55 : 60 : 65 : 70) cm
17¾ (19¾ : 21¾ : 23¾ : 25½ : 27½) in

BACK

With 3mm (US 2) needles and A cast on 74(82:90:98:106:114) sts.

1st rib row P3, [k4, p4] to last 7 sts, k4, p3.

2nd rib row P to end.

Rep the last 2 rows 6(6:7:7:8:8) times more.

Change to 3.25mm (US 3) needles and M.

Beg with a k row, cont in st st.

Work 58(58:60:60:62:62) rows.

Dec row K4, skpo, k to last 6 sts, k2 tog, k4.

Work 9 rows.

Rep the last 10 rows 2(3:4:5:6:7) times more, and then the dec row again. 66(72:78:84:90:96) sts.

Cont in st st until back measures 33(37:41:45:49:53)cm/ 13(14½:16¼:17¾:19¼:21)in from cast on edge, ending with a p row.

Shape raglan armholes

Cast off 4 sts at beg of next 2 rows. 58(64:70:76:82:88) sts.

Next row K1, skpo, k to last 3 sts, k2 tog, k1.

Next row P to end.

Next row K to end.

Next row P to end.

Rep the last 4 rows 4 times more. 48(54:60:66:72:78) sts **.

Next row K1, skpo, k to last 3 sts, k2 tog, k1.

Next row P to end.

Rep the last 2 rows 8(10:12:14:16:18) times more. 30(32:34:36:38:40) sts.

Leave these sts on a holder.

FRONT

Work as given for back to **.

Next row K1, skpo, k to last 3 sts, k2 tog, k1.

Next row P to end.

Rep the last 2 rows 1(3:5:7:9:11) times more. 44(46:48:50:52:54) sts.

Shape front neck

Next row K1, skpo, k11, k2 tog, k1, turn and work on these sts for first side of front neck.

Next row P to end.

Next row K1, skpo, k to last 3 sts, k2 tog, k1.

Next row P to end.

Rep the last 2 rows 4 times more. 5 sts.

Next row K1, sl 1, k2 tog, psso, k1.

Next row P to end.

Leave these 3 sts on a holder.

With right side facing, slip centre 10(12:14:16:18:20) sts onto a holder, rejoin yarn to rem sts, k1, skpo, k11, k2 tog, k1.

Next row P to end.

Next row K1, skpo, k to last 3 sts, k2 tog, k1.

Next row P to end.

Rep the last 2 rows 4 times more. 5 sts.

Next row K1, k3 tog, k1.

Next row P to end.

Leave these 3 sts on a holder.

SLEEVES

With 3mm (US 2) needles and A cast on 42(42:47:47:52:52) sts.

1st rib row P2, [k3, p2] to end.

2nd rib row K2, [p3, k2] to end.

Rep the last 2 rows 5(5:6:6:7:7) times more, inc –(3:1:4:2:5) sts evenly across last row. 42(45:48:51:54:57) sts.

Change to 3.25mm (US 3) needles and B.

Beg with a k row, cont in st st.

Work 2 rows.

Inc row K3, m1, k to last 3 sts, m1, k3.

Work 5 rows.

Rep the last 6 rows 4(5:6:7:8:9) times more, and then the inc row again. 54(59:64:69:74:79) sts.

Cont straight until sleeve measures 21(24:26:28:31:34)cm/ 8¼(9½:10¼:11:12¼:13½)in from cast on edge, ending with a p row.

Shape sleeve top

Cast off 4 sts at beg of next 2 rows. 46(51:56:61:66:71) sts.

Next row K2, skpo, k to last 4 sts, k2 tog, k2.

Next row P to end.

Next row K to end.

Next row P to end.

Rep the last 4 rows 2(3:4:5:6:7) times more. 40(43:46:49:52:55) sts.

Next row K2, skpo, k to last 4 sts, k2 tog, k2.

Next row P to end.

Rep the last 2 rows until 14(17:20:23:26:29) sts rem, ending with a p row.

Leave these sts on a holder.

COLLAR

With 3.25mm (US 3) circular needle and A, k3 from left front holder, pick up and k14 sts down left side of front neck, k10(12:14:16:18:20) sts from centre front holder, pick up and k13 sts up right side of front neck, k2 from holder, k last st on holder tog with first st on right sleeve, k12(15:18:21:24:27), k last st tog with first st on back, k28(30:32:34:36:38), k last st on back tog with first st on left sleeve, k13(16:19:22:25:28) from left sleeve, turn, cast on 6 sts for buttonband. 104(114:124:134:144:154) sts.

Work backwards and forwards in rows.

1st row (right side of collar) K6, [p2, k3] to last 8 sts, p2, k6.

2nd row K1, p5, [k2, p3] to last 8 sts, k2, p5, k1.

These 2 rows form the rib.

Work a further 4 rows.

Buttonhole row Rib to last 6 sts, k2 tog, y2rn, skpo, k2.

Rib 9(9:9:11:11:11) rows.

Rep the last 10(10:10:12:12:12) rows twice more, and then the buttonhole row again.

Rib 5 rows.

Cast off loosely in rib.

TO MAKE UP

Join raglan seams. Join side and sleeve seams. Catch cast on edge of buttonband to neck edge. Sew on buttons.

INVOLVEMENT

**WHY NOT GET THE WEARER OF THE DRESS TO CHOOSE
HER FAVOURITE COLOURS?**

LINDGREN MITTENS

SKILL LEVEL IMPROVING

SIZES
To fit age   1–2   2–3   3–4   years

MATERIALS
Heart mittens
One 50g/1¾oz ball of MillaMia Naturally Soft Merino in Scarlet (140) (M).
One ball of Snow (124) (C).
Snowflake mittens
One 50g/1¾oz ball of MillaMia Naturally Soft Merino in Seaside (161) (M).
One ball of Snow (124) (C).
Stripe garter stitch mittens
One 50g/1¾oz ball of MillaMia Naturally Soft Merino in each of
Forget me not (120) (M) and Putty Grey (121) (C).
Plain garter stitch mittens
One 50g/1¾oz ball of MillaMia Naturally Soft Merino in Berry (163).
All versions
Pair of 3.25mm (US 3) knitting needles.
Set of 3.25mm (US 3) double pointed needles.

TENSION / GAUGE
25 sts and 34 rows to 10cm/4in square over st st using
3.25mm (US 3) needles.
25 sts and 50 rows to 10cm/4in square over g-st using
3.25mm (US 3) needles.

HINTS AND TIPS
These are a great gift for any little ones in your family.
The blunt, loose shape makes them nice and easy to
slip on and the i-cord helps stop them from dropping
off. Note that the thumbs on these sweet mittens are
in stocking stitch for all versions.

ABBREVIATIONS
See page 11.

ALTERNATIVE COLOURWAYS

Fuchsia   Snow   Midnight Snow   Daisy   Snow   Scarlet   Snow
143   124   101   124   Yellow   124   140   124
                                        142

7 (8 : 9) cm
2¾ (3 : 3½) in

12 (15 : 17) cm
4¾ (6 : 6¾) in

HEART MITTENS

RIGHT MITTEN

With 3.25mm (US 3) needles and M cast on 32(36:40) sts.
Rib row [K1, p1] to end.
Rep the last row 11(13:15) times more.
Beg with a k row, cont in st st.
Work 4(6:8) rows.
Thumb opening
1st row K18(20:22), turn and cast on one st, work on these sts for back, leave rem 14(16:18) sts on a spare needle for front.
Work a further 1(3:3) rows.
Place Heart Motif
1st row Using M, k2(3:4), work across 1st row of Heart Motif Chart, using M, k4(5:6).
2nd row Using M, p4(5:6), work across 2nd row of Heart Motif Chart, using M, p2(3:4).
These 2 rows set the Chart.
Work a further 4(6:8) rows, ending with a wrong side row.
Next row Patt to end, cast on one st.
Break off yarn.
With right side facing, rejoin yarn to rem sts, cast on one st, k to end.
15(17:19) sts.
Work 7(11:13) rows, ending with a wrong side row.
Next row Cast on one st, k to end.
Next row P to end, then patt across sts of back. 36(40:44) sts.
Work 10(12:14) rows, working in M only when Chart is completed.
Shape top
Next row K2, [skpo, k11(13:15), k2 tog, k2] twice.
P 1 row.
Next row K2, [skpo, k9(11:13), k2 tog, k2] twice.
P 1 row.
Next row K2, [skpo, k7(9:11), k2 tog, k2] twice.
P 1 row.
Cast off.

HEART MOTIF CHART

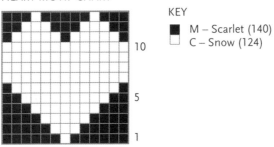

KEY
■ M – Scarlet (140)
☐ C – Snow (124)

LEFT MITTEN

With 3.25mm (US 3) needles and M cast on 32(36:40) sts.

Rib row [K1, p1] to end.

Rep the last row 11(13:15) times more.

Beg with a k row, cont in st st.

Work 4(6:8) rows.

Thumb opening

1st row K14(16:18), turn and cast on one st, work on these sts for front, leave rem 18(20:22) sts on a spare needle for back.

Work 7(11:13) rows, ending with a wrong side row.

Next row K to end, cast on one st.

Break off yarn.

With right side facing, rejoin yarn to rem sts, cast on one st, k to end. 19(21:23) sts.

Work a further 1(3:3) rows.

Place Heart Motif

1st row Using M, k4(5:6), work across 1st row of Heart Motif Chart, using M, k2(3:4).

2nd row Using M, p2(3:4), work across 2nd row of Heart Motif Chart, using M, p4(5:6).

These 2 rows set the Chart.

Work a further 4(6:8) rows, ending with a wrong side row.

Next row Cast on one st, patt to end.

Next row Patt to end, then p across sts of front. 36(40:44) sts.

Work 10(12:14) rows, working in M only when Chart is completed.

Shape top

Next row K2, [skpo, k11(13:15), k2 tog, k2] twice.

P 1 row.

Next row K2, [skpo, k9(11:13), k2 tog, k2] twice.

P 1 row.

Next row K2, [skpo, k7(9:11), k2 tog, k2] twice.

P 1 row.

Cast off.

THUMB (Make 2)

With 3.25mm (US 3) needles and M cast on 2 sts.

Beg with a k row, work in st st.

Work 2 rows.

Shape sides

1st row Inc in first st, m1, k1. 4 sts.

Work 3 rows.

Inc row K1, m1, k to last st, m1, k1.

Work 3 rows.

Rep the last 4 rows –(1:1) times more, and then the first 2(2:4) rows again. 8(10:10) sts.

Cast on 2 sts at beg of next 2 rows. 12(14:14) sts.

Mark each end of last row with a coloured thread.

Work 8(10:12) rows.

Shape top

Next row [K2 tog] 6(7:7) times.

Next row P to end.

Break off yarn, thread though rem sts and secure, then join seam to coloured threads.

CORD

With 3.25mm (US 3) double pointed needles and M cast on 3 sts.

1st row [Inc in next st] twice. 6 sts. Do not turn, bring yarn across back of work to beg of row.

2nd row K to end, do not turn, bring yarn across back of work to beg of row.

Rep the last row until cord measures 70(80:90)cm/ 27½(31½:35½)in.

[Work 2 tog] 3 times, thread yarn through rem sts and fasten off.

TO MAKE UP

Sew thumb into thumb opening. Fold mitten in half and join top and side seam. Sew cord to mittens.

SNOWFLAKE MITTENS

Work as given for Heart Mittens, but work from Snowflake Motif Chart.

SNOWFLAKE MOTIF CHART

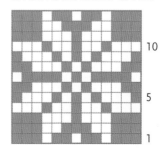

KEY

M – Seaside (161)
C – Snow (124)

STRIPE GARTER STITCH MITTENS

RIGHT MITTEN
With 3.25mm (US 3) needles and M cast on 32(36:40) sts.
Rib row [K1, p1] to end.
Rep the last row 12(14:16) times more.
Work in g-st and stripes of 1 row M, then [2 rows C, 2 rows M] throughout.
Work 5(7:9) rows.

Thumb opening
1st row K18(20:22), turn and cast on one st, work on these sts for back, leave rem 14(16:18) sts on a spare needle for front.
Work a further 15(17:19) rows, ending with a wrong side row.
Next row K to end, cast on one st.
Break off yarn.
With right side facing, rejoin yarn to rem sts, cast on one st, k to end. 15(17:19) sts.
Work a further 15(17:19) rows, ending with a wrong side row.
Next row Cast on one st, k to end.
Next row K to end, then k across sts of back.
36(40:44) sts.
K 14(16:18) rows.

Shape top
Next row K2, [skpo, k11(13:15), k2 tog, k2] twice.
K 2 rows.
Next row K2, [skpo, k9(11:13), k2 tog, k2] twice.
K 2 rows.
Next row K2, [skpo, k7(9:11), k2 tog, k2] twice.
K 1 row.
Cast off.

LEFT MITTEN
With 3.25mm (US 3) needles and M cast on 32(36:40) sts.
Rib row [K1, p1] to end.
Rep the last row 12(14:16) times more.
Work in g-st and stripes of 1 row M, then [2 rows C, 2 rows M] throughout.
Work 5(7:9) rows.

Thumb opening
1st row K14(16:18), turn and cast on one st, work on these sts for front, leave rem 18(20:22) sts on a spare needle for back.
Work a further 15(17:19) rows, ending with a wrong side row.
Next row K to end, cast on one st.
Break off yarn.
With right side facing, rejoin yarn to rem sts, cast on one st, k to end. 19(21:23) sts.
Work a further 15(17:19) rows, ending with a wrong side row.
Next row Cast on one st, k to end.
Next row K to end, then k across sts of front.
36(40:44) sts.
K 14(16:18) rows.

Shape top
Next row K2, [skpo, k11(13:15), k2 tog, k2] twice.
K 2 rows.
Next row K2, [skpo, k9(11:13), k2 tog, k2] twice.
K 2 rows.
Next row K2, [skpo, k7(9:11), k2 tog, k2] twice.
K 1 row.
Cast off.

TO COMPLETE
Work thumbs and cord and make up as given for Heart Mittens.

PLAIN GARTER STITCH MITTENS

Work as given for Stripe Garter Stitch Mittens, working in one colour throughout.

KRISTER BOOTIES

SKILL LEVEL BEGINNER / IMPROVING

SIZES

To fit age   3–6 months

MATERIALS

One 50g/1¾oz ball of MillaMia Naturally Soft Merino in each of
Fuchsia (143) (A), Daisy Yellow (142) (B) and Peacock (144) (C).
Pair of 2.75mm (US 2) knitting needles.

TENSION / GAUGE

28 sts and 50 rows to 10cm/4in square over g-st using
2.75mm (US 2) needles.

HINTS AND TIPS

Small and sweet, these make the perfect gift for any new parents.
Who says babies need to be dressed in lemon yellow and pastels!
These booties are a quick knit and make a good introduction to more
complex shaping for the new knitter.

ABBREVIATIONS

See page 11.

ALTERNATIVE COLOURWAYS

Scarlet Midnight Snow
140   101   124

Berry   Plum Seaside
163   162   161

Putty Daisy Storm
Grey Yellow 102
121   142

Seaside Claret Fawn
161   104   160

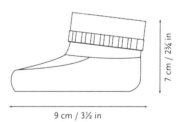

7 cm / 2¾ in

9 cm / 3½ in

FOR HIM, FOR HER

THESE WORK EQUALLY AS WELL FOR LITTLE BOYS AND GIRLS.

UPPER SECTIONS (Make 2)

With 2.75mm (US 2) needles and A cast on 38 sts.

1st rib row K2, [p2, k2] to end.

2nd rib row P2, [k2, p2] to end.

These 2 rows form the rib.

Work a further 4 rows, dec 2 sts evenly across last row. 36 sts.

K 30 rows.

Break off A.

Shape instep

Slip first 13 sts onto a holder, rejoin B to next st, k10, turn and work on these 10 sts.

Work 23 rows in g-st on centre 10 sts.

Next row K1, skpo, k to last 3 sts, k2 tog, k1.

K 1 row.

Rep the last 2 rows once more. 6 sts.

Break off B.

With right side facing and using C, k13 sts from holder, pick up and k14 sts along side of instep, k across centre 6 sts, then pick up and k14 sts along other side of instep, k13. 60 sts.

K 12 rows.

Cast off.

SOLES (Make 2)

With 2.75mm (US 2) needles and A cast on 4 sts.

K 1 row.

Next row Cast on 2 sts, k to end.

Rep the last row 3 times more. 12 sts.

K 34 rows.

Next row K1, skpo, k to last 3 sts, k2 tog, k1.

K 1 row.

Rep the last 2 rows twice more. 6 sts.

Cast off.

TO MAKE UP

Join back seam, reversing at top edge for turnover. With centre of cast on edge towards back seam and centre of cast off edge towards centre of upper boot, sew sole in place.

ASTRID CAP GLOVES

SKILL LEVEL IMPROVING

SIZES
To fit   Small to medium (medium to large) hands

MATERIALS
1(1) 50g/1¾oz ball of MillaMia Naturally Soft Merino in each of Daisy
Yellow (142) (A), Fuchsia (143) (B) and Peacock (144) (C).
Pair each of 3mm (US 2) and 3.25mm (US 3) knitting needles.
Small crochet hook.
2 buttons approx 12mm/½in in diameter.

TENSION / GAUGE
25 sts and 34 rows to 10cm square over st st using
3.25mm (US 3) needles.

HINTS AND TIPS
For a man you should make the second size of these gloves. A crochet
chain stitch is used to make the small button loop that later allows you
to hook the cap of the gloves securely in place when not in use.

ABBREVIATIONS
ch – chain.
See also page 11.

ALTERNATIVE COLOURWAYS

Peacock Midnight Scarlet
144   101   140

Storm   Snow   Pitch
102   124   Black
                      100

Forget   Fawn   Sable
me not   160   105
120

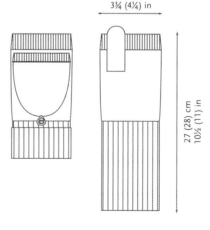

9.5 (11) cm
3¾ (4¼) in

27 (28) cm
10½ (11) in

RIGHT GLOVE

** With 3.25mm (US 3) needles and A cast 42(50) sts.

1st rib row K2, [p2, k2] to end.

2nd rib row P2, [k2, p2] to end.

These 2 rows form the rib.

Work a further 26 rows.

Change to 3mm (US 2) needles.

Work a further 27 rows.

Next row Rib to end, inc 8 sts evenly across last row. 50(58) sts.

Change to 3.25mm (US 3) needles and B.

Beg with a k row, cont in st st.

Work 16(18) rows **.

Thumb opening

Next row K26(30), cast off 9 sts, k to end.

Next row P15(19), cast on 9 sts, p to end.

*** Work a further 14(16) rows.

Work 6 rows in rib.

Cast off in rib.

Thumb

With 3.25mm (US 3) needles and C cast on 20 sts.

Beg with a k row, work 18 rows in st st.

Shape top

1st row K2, [k2 tog, k1] to end.

2nd row P to end.

3rd row K2, [k2 tog] to end. 8 sts.

Break off yarn, thread through rem sts and fasten off securely.

Join seam.

Cap top

With 3.25mm (US 3) needles and A cast on 54(62) sts.

1st rib row K2, [p2, k2] to end.

2nd rib row P2, [k2, p2] to end.

These 2 rows form the rib.

Work a further 6 rows.

Change to C.

Beg with a k row, work 18(20) rows in st st.

Shape top

1st row K2, skpo, k20(24), k2 tog, k2, skpo, k20(24), k2 tog, k2.

2nd row P to end.

3rd row K2, skpo, k18(22), k2 tog, k2, skpo, k18(22), k2 tog, k2.

4th row P to end.

5th row K2, skpo, k16(20), k2 tog, k2, skpo, k16(20), k2 tog, k2.

6th row P to end.

7th row K2, skpo, k14(18), k2 tog, k2, skpo, k14(18), k2 tog, k2.

8th row P to end.

9th row K2, skpo, k12(16), k2 tog, k2, skpo, k12(16), k2 tog, k2.

10th row P to end. 34(42) sts.

2nd size only

11th row K2, skpo, k–(14), k2 tog, k2, skpo, k–(14), k2 tog, k2.

12th row P to end. –(38) sts ***.

Both sizes

Cast off row Cast off 9(10) sts, slip last st onto crochet hook, make 5 ch, slip last loop back onto left hand needle, cast off to end.

LEFT GLOVE

Work as given for right glove from ** to **.

Thumb opening

Next row K15(19), cast off 9 sts, k to end.

Next row P26(30), cast on 9 sts, p to end.

Work as given for right glove from *** to ***.

Both sizes

Cast off row Cast off 25(28) sts, slip last st onto crochet hook, make 5 ch, slip last loop back onto left hand needle, cast off to end.

TO MAKE UP

Sew thumb to thumb opening. Join side seam, reversing at cuff for turnover. Fold cap in half and join top and side seam. Attach cap to back of glove. Sew on buttons to match buttonloops.

SILHOUETTE WRAPPING PAPER

ONE OF THE THINGS WE LOVE ABOUT KNITTING AND KNITTED FABRICS IS THE AMOUNT OF TEXTURE YOU CAN CREATE. DESIGNING KNITWEAR THEREFORE BECOMES A WONDERFUL THREE-DIMENSIONAL EXPERIENCE RATHER THAN JUST THINKING ABOUT SHAPING AND COLOURS. THE LOVE OF LACE AND KNITTED TEXTURES HAS HELPED HELENA COME UP WITH THIS INSPIRING IDEA FOR WRAPPING PAPER – COMBINING HER PASSION FOR PRINT-BASED PATTERNS WITH THE RICH TEXTURES OF KNITTED DESIGNS. WE HOPE YOU HAVE AS MUCH FUN COMING UP WITH YOUR OWN INIMITABLE GIFT WRAP. WHAT WE ADORE IS THE WAY THIS TECHNIQUE OF TRANSFERRING THE PATTERN TO THE WRAPPING PAPER LEAVES BEHIND JUST AN ECHO OR SILHOUETTE OF WHAT IT ONCE WAS.

SILHOUETTE WRAPPING PAPER

SIZES / MEASUREMENTS

Makes several 70cm/27½in by 50cm/19¾in sheets of wrapping paper.

MATERIALS

Lace or textured knitwear; you can use a whole garment or fabric pieces and trimmings.

70cm/27½in by 50cm/19¾in sheets of wrapping paper in your choice of colour.

Spray paint suitable for use on paper in your choice of colour.

Old newspapers to protect your work area.

NOTE

If you have some old clothes in the wardrobe that you never wear, this is a great chance to put them to use. Or scour charity shops for old garments that are out of fashion but have interesting patterns and textures – it's time for them to be reinvented into a new life. The spray paint and paper can easily be found online or in any good art shop. You can choose any colour wrapping paper you like, but bear in mind that it is easier to spray dark colours onto a lighter background.

TO MAKE

1 Cover the floor/table area where you are working with newspaper. Open any windows and doors to ensure a well-ventilated space when working with spray paint.

2 Place your wrapping paper on the newspaper and position the fabric on top as desired. Using the outline of a garment (that is, the edges of the garment) can look quite effective on large packages, but you can just place it as you like. Lay the fabric as flat to the wrapping paper as possible (it can be wise to iron it first to help with this).

3 Keeping everything as still as possible (anchor the fabric in place with masking tape if necessary), spray your chosen colour paint directly from above. Make sure that you fill all areas of paper not covered by the fabric.

4 Allow the paint to dry completely before removing the fabric and unveiling your design on the paper.

COMFORT

WEARABLE WOOLLENS, SOFT AND LUXURIOUS –
NOTHING CAN MATCH THE COMFORTING FEEL OF
SLIPPING INTO A PAIR OF HAND KNITTED SOCKS
OR A COSY CARDIGAN. ENJOY.

DANIEL CARDIGAN

SKILL LEVEL IMPROVING

DANIEL CARDIGAN

SKILL LEVEL EXPERIENCED

SIZES / MEASUREMENTS

To fit bust/chest	87–92	97–102	107–112	117–122	cm
	34–36	38–40	42–44	46–48	in

ACTUAL MEASUREMENTS

Bust/chest	96	106	116	125	cm
	38	41¾	45¾	49	in
Length to shoulder	65	67	69	71	cm
	25½	26½	27¼	28	in

Sleeve length (woman's version)	46cm/18in for all sizes
Sleeve length (man's version)	50cm/19¾in for all sizes

MATERIALS

15(17:19:21) 50g/1¾oz balls of MillaMia Naturally Soft Merino in Midnight (101) (M).
Two balls of Snow (124) (C).
Pair each of 3mm (US 2) and 3.25mm (US 3) knitting needles.
8 buttons approx 12mm/½in in diameter.

TENSION / GAUGE

25 sts and 34 rows to 10cm/4in square over st st using 3.25mm(US 3) needles.

HINTS AND TIPS

Wear as a relaxed-fit, boyfriend-style cardigan for women and as an on-trend Fair Isle piece for men.

ABBREVIATIONS

See page 11.

ALTERNATIVE COLOURWAYS

Storm Midnight
102   101

Putty   Snow
Grey   124
121

Claret   Storm
104   102

48 (53 : 58 : 62.5) cm
19 (21 : 23 : 24½) in

man's version:
50 cm/19¾ in
woman's version:
46 cm / 18 in

65 (67 : 69 : 71) cm
25½ (26½ : 27¼ : 28) in

A BOYFRIEND CARDIGAN

CAN SOMETIMES BE WORN BY THE BOYFRIEND, TOO!

NOTE

If making the woman's version, knit the back and then left front first and mark positions for 6 buttons: the first 5cm/2in from cast on edge, the sixth 3cm/1¼in from beg of neck shaping and the rem 4 spaced evenly between.

Work buttonholes on right front to match markers as folls:

Buttonhole row (right side) K4, p1, k1, p1, k2 tog, y2rn, skpo, patt to end.

If making the man's version, knit the back and then right front first and mark positions for 6 buttons: the first 5cm/2in from cast on edge, the sixth 3cm/1¼in from beg of neck shaping and the rem 4 spaced evenly between.

Work buttonholes on left front to match markers as folls:

Buttonhole row (right side) Patt to last 11 sts, k2 tog, y2rn, skpo, p1, k1, p1, k4.

BACK

With 3mm (US 2) needles and M cast on 123(135:147:159) sts.
1st row K1, [p1, k1] to end.
2nd row P1, [k1, p1] to end.
Rep the last 2 rows 9 times more.
Change to 3.25mm (US 3) needles.
Beg with a k row, work in st st until back measures 25(26:27:28)cm/10(10¼:10½:11)in from cast on edge, ending with a p row.

Work from Chart
1st row K2 sts before patt rep, [work across 4 st patt rep] 30(33:36:39) times, k1 st after patt rep.
2nd row P1 st before patt rep, [work across 4 st patt rep] 30(33:36:39) times, p2 sts after patt rep.
These 2 rows set the patt for the Chart.
Continue in patt until back measures 43(44:45:46)cm/17(17¼:17¾:18) in from cast on edge, ending with a p row.

Shape armholes
Cast off 8 sts at beg of next 2 rows. 107(119:131:143) sts.
Cont in patt to end of Chart then work in M only until back measures 65(67:69:71)cm/25½(26½:27¼:28)in, ending with a p row.

Shape shoulders
Cast off 8(9:10:11) sts at beg of next 8 rows.
Cast off rem 43(47:51:55) sts.

RIGHT FRONT

With 3mm (US 2) needles and M cast on 73(81:89:97) sts.
1st row K4, p1, [k1, p1] to end.
2nd row [K1, p1] to last 3 sts, k3.
Rep the last 2 rows 9 times more.
Change to 3.25mm (US 3) needles.
1st row (right side) K4, [p1, k1] 5 times, p1, k to end.
2nd row P to last 15 sts, [k1, p1] 6 times, k3.

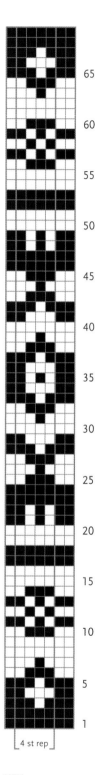

KEY
■ M – Midnight (101)
□ C – Snow (124)

These 2 rows form the st st with rib border.

Work straight until front measures 25(26:27:28)cm/10(10¼:10½:11)in from cast on edge, ending with a wrong side row.

Work from Chart

1st row Using M, k4, [p1, k1] 5 times, p1, k1 st before patt rep, [work across 4 st patt rep] 14(16:18:20) times, k1 st after patt rep.

2nd row P1 st before patt rep, [work across 4 st patt rep] 14(16:18:20) times, p1 st after patt rep, using M, [k1, p1] 6 times, k3.

These 2 rows set the patt for the Chart and front rib.

Continue in patt until front measures 43(44:45:46)cm/17(17¼:17¾:18) in from cast on edge, ending with a right side row.

Shape armhole

Next row Cast off 8 sts, patt to end. 65(73:81:89) sts.

Shape front neck

1st row Rib 15 sts, place these sts onto a holder, patt to end. 50(58:66:74) sts.

Cont in patt to end of Chart then work in M only, **at the same time** dec one st at neck edge on 6(12:18:24) foll right side rows, then 12(10:8:6) foll 4th rows. 32(36:40:44) sts.

Work straight until front measures the same as back to shoulder, ending at armhole edge.

Shape shoulder

Cast off 8(9:10:11) sts at beg of next and 2 foll wrong side rows.

Work 1 row.

Cast off rem 8(9:10:11) sts.

LEFT FRONT

With 3mm (US 2) needles and M cast on 73(81:89:97) sts.

1st row P1, [k1, p1] to last 4 sts, k4.

2nd row K3, [p1, k1] to end.

Rep the last 2 rows 9 times more.

Change to 3.25mm (US 3) needles.

1st row (right side) K to last 15 sts, p1, [k1, p1] 5 times, k4.

2nd row K3, [p1, k1] 6 times, p to end.

These 2 rows form the st st with rib border.

Work straight until front measures 25(26:27:28)cm/10(10¼:10½:11)in from cast on edge, ending with a wrong side row.

Work from Chart

1st row K1 st before patt rep, [work across 4 st patt rep] 14(16:18:20) times, k1 st after patt rep, using M, p1, [k1, p1] 5 times, k4.

2nd row Using M, k3, [p1, k1] 6 times, p1 st before patt rep, [work across 4 st patt rep] 14(16:18:20) times, p1 st after patt rep.

These 2 rows set the patt for the Chart and front rib.

Continue in patt until front measures 43(44:45:46)cm/17(17¼:17¾:18) in from cast on edge, ending with a wrong side row.

Shape armhole

Next row Cast off 8 sts, patt to end. 65(73:81:89) sts.

Patt 1 row.

Shape front neck

1st row Patt to last 15 sts, place these 15 sts onto a holder.
50(58:66:74) sts.

Cont in patt to end of Chart then work in M only, **at the same time** dec one st at neck edge on 6(12:18:24) foll right side rows, then 12(10:8:6) foll 4th rows. 32(36:40:44) sts.

Work straight until front measures the same as back to shoulder, ending at armhole edge.

Shape shoulder

Cast off 8(9:10:11) sts at beg of next and 2 foll right side rows.

Work 1 row.

Cast off rem 8(9:10:11) sts.

SLEEVES

With 3mm (US 2) needles and M cast on 65(71:77:83) sts.

1st row K1, [p1, k1] to end.

2nd row P1, [k1, p1] to end.

Woman's version

Rep the last 2 rows 7 times more.

Man's version

Rep the last 2 rows 9 times more.

Both versions

Change to 3.25mm (US 3) needles.

Beg with a k row, work in st st.

Work 4 rows.

1st inc row K3, m1, k to last 3 sts, m1, k3.

Work 6 rows.

2nd inc row P3, m1p, p to last 3 sts, m1p, p3.

Work 6 rows.

Woman's version

Rep the last 14 rows 8 times more, and then the first 8 rows again. 105(111:117:123) sts.

Cont straight until sleeve measures 46cm/18in from cast on edge, ending with a p row.

Mark each end of last row with a coloured thread.

Work a further 10 rows.

Cast off 8 sts at beg of next 10 rows. 25(31:37:43) sts.

Cast off.

Man's version

Rep the last 14 rows 9 times more, and then the 1st inc row again. 107(113:119:125) sts.

Cont straight until sleeve measures 50cm/19¾in from cast on edge, ending with a p row.

Mark each end of last row with a coloured thread.

Work a further 10 rows.

Cast off 8 sts at beg of next 10 rows. 27(33:39:45) sts.

Cast off.

POCKETS (MAKE 2)

With 3.25mm (US 3) needles and M cast on 37(39:41:41) sts.
Beg with a k row, work 39(41:43:45) rows in st st.
Pocket top
1st row K3, [p1, k1] to last 4 sts, p1, k3.
2nd row K3, p to last 3 sts, k3.
Rep the last 2 rows 3 times more.
Next row (buttonhole row) Rib 16(17:18:18), work 2 tog, y2rn,
work 2 tog, rib to end.
Work a further 7 rows.
Cast off in rib.

LEFT COLLAR

With right side facing, place 15 sts from holder onto a 3.25mm (US 3)
needle, using M, rib to end.
Next row Patt to end.
Inc one st at inside edge of every row until there are 63 sts.
Next row Patt to end.
Next 2 rows K3, [p1, k1] 16 times, turn, rib to end.
Rib 4 rows across all sts.
Rep the last 6 rows until inside edge fits up left front and halfway across
back neck.
Cast off.

RIGHT COLLAR

With wrong side facing, place 15 sts from holder onto a 3.25mm (US 3)
needle, using M, rib to end.
Next row Rib to end.
Inc one st at inside edge of every row until there are 63 sts.
Next row Patt to end.
Next 2 rows K4, [p1, k1] 15 times, p1, turn, rib to end.
Rib 4 rows across all sts.
Rep the last 6 rows until inside edge fits up left front and halfway across
back neck.
Cast off.

TO MAKE UP

Join shoulder seams. Join cast off edges of collar. Sew collar to neck
edge. Join side and sleeve seams. Sew in sleeves, with rows above
coloured threads to sts cast off at underarm. Sew on pockets as far as
pocket top, fold top onto right side and sew on buttons.

MY SOCKS

SKILL LEVEL IMPROVING

SIZE
To fit an average adult woman's foot – knit according to your desired length.

MATERIALS
Three 50g/1¾oz balls of MillaMia Naturally Soft Merino in Fawn (160).
Set each of 3mm (US 2) and 3.75mm (US 5) double pointed needles.
Cable needle.
Stitch markers.
Tapestry needle.

TENSION / GAUGE
32 sts and 34 rows to 10cm/4in square over patt using 3.75mm (US 5) needles.

HINTS AND TIPS
The toes on these socks are grafted together using Kitchener stitch. This technique joins two sets of stitches that are still on the needle (so 'live' stitches) by using a tapestry needle threaded with yarn to create a row that looks like knit stitches between them. There are plenty of tutorials online, including on the MillaMia blog, to learn this technique should you need help.

ABBREVIATIONS
C2F, cable 2 front – slip next st onto cable needle and hold at front of work, k1, then k1 from cable needle.
C2B, cable 2 back – slip next st onto cable needle and hold at back of work, k1, then k1 from cable needle.
See also page 11.

ALTERNATIVE COLOURWAYS

Berry
163

Plum
162

Putty
Grey
121

Snow
124

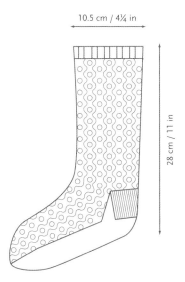

10.5 cm / 4¼ in

28 cm / 11 in

SOCKS

With 3mm (US 2) needles cast on 68 sts.

Arrange these sts on 3 needles and cont in rnds.

Next rnd K1 tbl, * p2, [k1 tbl] twice; rep from * to last 3 sts, p2, k1 tbl.

Rep the last rnd 8 times more.

Change to 3.75mm (US 5) needles.

1st rnd K to end.

2nd rnd [C2F, C2B] to end.

3rd rnd K to end.

4th rnd [C2B, C2F] to end.

These 4 rnds set the patt.

Cont in patt until leg measures 20cm/8in, ending with a 2nd or 4th rnd.

Back heel

Foundation row K2, [k2 tog, k2] 3 times, k2 tog, k1, turn.

Next row Sl 1, p13, p2 tog, [p2, p2 tog] 3 times, p2. 26 sts.

Work on these 26 sts only.

Next row [Sl 1, k1] to end.

Next row Sl 1, p to end.

Working backwards and forwards on these 26 sts, work a further 23 rows.

Turn heel

1st row Sl 1, p14, p2 tog, p1, turn.

2nd row Sl 1, k5, ssk, k1, turn.

3rd row Sl 1, p6, p2 tog, p1, turn.

4th row Sl 1, k7, ssk, k1, turn.

5th row Sl 1, p8, p2 tog, p1, turn.

6th row Sl 1, k9, ssk, k1, turn.

7th row Sl 1, p10, p2 tog, p1, turn.

8th row Sl 1, k11, ssk, k1, turn.

9th row Sl 1, p12, p2 tog, p1, turn.

10th row Sl 1, k13, ssk, k1, do not turn. 16 sts.

Instep

Pick up and k1 st in each of the slipped sts along the first side of heel. 13 sts.

Pick up and k1 st between the side of heel and the top/instep sts, place a marker loop, k1, patt 32, k1 st of instep, place a marker loop, pick up and k1 st between instep sts and second side of heel, pick up and k1 st in each of the slipped sts along the second side of heel (13 sts), k first 8 sts from heel.

Dec rnd K to 3 sts before first marker, k2 tog, k1, sm, patt to next marker, sm, k1, ssk, k to end.

Next rnd K to marker, patt 34, k to end.

Rep the last 2 rnds until 60 sts rem.

Foot

Cont in patt until foot measures 4cm/1½in shorter than desired length.

Decrease for toe

Dec rnd K to 3 sts before first marker, k2 tog, k1, sm, [k1, ssk] 5 times, k4, [k2 tog, k1] 5 times, sm, k1, ssk, k to end. 48 sts.

K 1 rnd.

Next rnd K to 3 sts before first marker, k2 tog, k1, sm, k1, ssk, k to 3 sts before second marker, k2 tog, k1, sm, k1, ssk, k to end.

Rep the last 2 rnds until 20 sts rem.

K to first marker and arrange sts so that there are 10 sts on each of 2 needles.

Graft toe together using Kitchener stitch.

INGRID CARDIGAN

SKILL LEVEL IMPROVING

SIZES / MEASUREMENTS

To fit age	1–2	2–3	4–5	6–7	8–10	years

ACTUAL MEASUREMENTS

Chest	58	62	67	72	76	cm
	23	24½	26½	28½	30	in
Length to shoulder	28	32	36	40	44	cm
	11	12½	14¼	15¾	17¼	in
Sleeve length	21	24	26	28	32	cm
	8¼	9½	10¼	11	12½	in

MATERIALS

5 (6:6:7:8) 50g/1¾oz balls of MillaMia Naturally Soft Merino in Snow (124).
Pair each of 3mm (US 2) and 3.25mm (US 3) knitting needles.
Circular 3mm (US 2) knitting needle.
6 buttons approx 12mm/½in in diameter.

TENSION / GAUGE

25 sts and 34 rows to 10cm/4in square over st st using
3.25mm (US 3) needles.
30 sts and 40 rows to 10cm/4in square over Irish moss st using
3.25mm (US 3) needles.

HINTS AND TIPS

We love teaming this pretty, soft cardigan with a beautiful dress although
we think it would look equally as cool with jeans and boots. Irish moss stitch
is a double moss stitch that gives a lovely, unusual diagonal texture.

ABBREVIATIONS

See page 11.

ALTERNATIVE COLOURWAYS

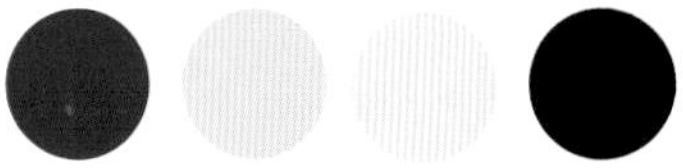

Scarlet
140

Forget
me not
120

Petal
122

Claret
104

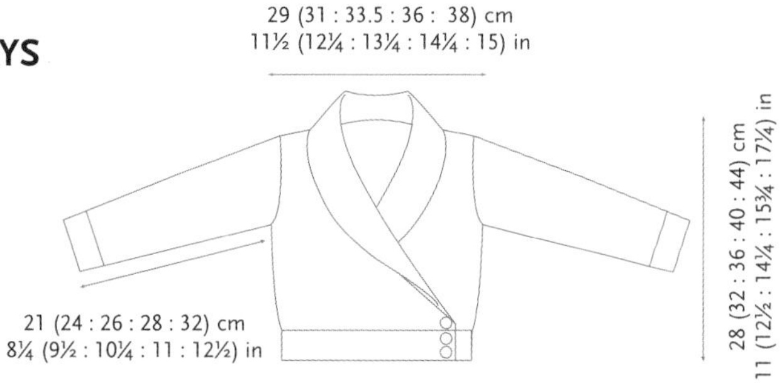

29 (31 : 33.5 : 36 : 38) cm
11½ (12¼ : 13¼ : 14¼ : 15) in

21 (24 : 26 : 28 : 32) cm
8¼ (9½ : 10¼ : 11 : 12½) in

28 (32 : 36 : 40 : 44) cm
11 (12½ : 14¼ : 15¾ : 17¼) in

BACK

With 3mm (US 2) needles cast on 74(80:86:92:98) sts.

Rib row [K1, p1] to end.

Rep the last row 17 times more.

Change to 3.25mm (US 3) needles.

Beg with a k row, cont in st st until back measures 16(19:22:25:28)cm/6¼(7½:8¾:10:11)in from cast on edge, ending with a p row.

Shape armholes

Cast off 3(3:4:4:5) sts at beg of next 2 rows. 68(74:78:84:88) sts.

Next row K2, skpo, k to last 4 sts, k2 tog, k2.

Next row P to end.

Rep the last 2 rows 5(6:6:7:7) times more. 56(60:64:68:72) sts.

Cont in st st until back measures 28(32:36:40:44)cm/11(12½:14¼:15¾:17¼)in from cast on edge, ending with a p row.

Shape shoulders

Cast off 6(7:7:8:8) sts at beg of next 2 rows and 7(7:8:8:9) sts at beg of foll 2 rows.

Leave rem 30(32:34:36:38) sts on a holder.

LEFT FRONT

With 3mm (US 2) needles cast on 52(56:60:64:68) sts.

1st rib row [K1, p1] to last 2 sts, k2.

2nd rib row [K1, p1] to end.

These 2 rows form the rib.

Work a further 2 rows.

Buttonhole row Rib to last 4 sts, yon, k2 tog, k2.

Rib a further 11 rows.

Buttonhole row Rib to last 4 sts, yon, k2 tog, k2.

Inc row Rib 11(5:10:6:17), m1, [rib 5(5:4:4:3), m1] 7(9:11:13:15) times, rib 6. 60(66:72:78:84) sts.

Change to 3.25mm (US 3) needles.

1st row [K1, p1] to last 2 sts, k2.

2nd row [K1, p1] to end.

3rd row [P1, k1] to last 6 sts, p2, k1, p1, k2.

4th row [K1, p1] twice, k2, [p1, k1] to end.

These 4 rows form the Irish moss st with rib border.

Work a further 6 rows.

Buttonhole row Patt to last 5 sts, p1, yon, k2 tog, k2.

Work 3 more rows.

Shape front neck

Next row Work in Irish moss st to last 3 sts, k2 tog, k1.

Next row P2, work in Irish moss st to end.

Rep the last 2 rows until side seam measures the same as back to armhole shaping, ending at side edge.

Cont to dec at front edge, **at the same time** start shaping armhole.

Shape armhole

Next row Cast off 3(3:4:4:5) sts, patt to last 3 sts, k2 tog, k1.

Next row P2, patt to end.

Next row Skpo, patt to last 3 sts, k2 tog, k1.

Next row P2, patt to end.

Rep the last 2 rows 5(6:6:7:7) times more.

Keeping armhole edge straight, cont to dec at neck edge on every right side row until 15(16:17:18:19) sts rem.

Work straight until front matches back to shoulder, ending at armhole edge.

Shape shoulder

Cast off 7(8:8:9:9) sts at beg of next row.

Work 1 row.

Cast off rem 8(8:9:9:10) sts.

RIGHT FRONT

With 3mm (US 2) needles cast on 52(56:60:64:68) sts.

1st rib row K2, [p1, k1] to end.

2nd rib row [P1, k1] to end.

These 2 rows form the rib.

Work a further 2 rows.

Buttonhole row K2, k2 tog, yrn, rib to end.

Rib a further 11 rows.

Buttonhole row K2, k2 tog, yrn, rib to end.

Inc row Rib 6, m1, [rib 5(5:4:4:3), m1] 7(9:11:13:15) times, rib 11(5:10:6:17). 60(66:72:78:84) sts.

Change to 3.25mm (US 3) needles.

1st row K2, [p1, k1] to end.

2nd row [P1, k1] to end.

3rd row K2, p1, k1, p2, [k1, p1] to end.

4th row [K1, p1] to last 6 sts, k2, [p1, k1] twice.

These 4 rows form the Irish moss st with rib border.

Work a further 6 rows.

Buttonhole row K2, k2 tog, yrn, patt to end.

Work 3 more rows.

Shape front neck

Next row K1, skpo, work in Irish moss st to end.

Next row Work in Irish moss st to last 2 sts, p2.

Rep the last 2 rows until side seam measures the same as back to armhole shaping, ending at side edge.

Cont to dec at front edge, **at the same time** start shaping armhole.

Shape armhole

Next row Cast off 3(3:4:4:5) sts, patt to last 2 sts, p2.

Next row K1, skpo, patt to last 2 sts, k2 tog.

Next row Patt to last 2 sts, p2.

Rep the last 2 rows 5(6:6:7:7) times.

Keeping armhole edge straight, cont to dec at neck edge on every right side row until 15(16:17:18:19) sts rem.

Work straight until front matches back to shoulder, ending at armhole edge.

Shape shoulder

Cast off 7(8:8:9:9) sts at beg of next row.

Work 1 row.

Cast off rem 8(8:9:9:10) sts.

SLEEVES

With 3mm (US 2) needles cast on 41(43:45:47:49) sts.
1st rib row K1, [p1, k1] to end.
2nd rib row P1, [k1, p1] to end.
Rep the last 2 rows 5 times more.
Change to 3.25mm (US 3) needles.
Beg with a k row, cont in st st.
Work 2 rows.
Inc row K3, m1, k to last 3 sts, m1, k3.
Work 5 rows.
Rep the last 6 rows 6(7:8:9:10) times more, and then the inc row again.
57(61:65:69:73) sts.
Cont straight until sleeve measures 21(24:26:28:32)cm/8¼(9½:10¼:
11:12½)in from cast on edge, ending with a p row.
Shape sleeve top
Cast off 3(3:4:4:5) sts at beg of next 2 rows. 51(55:57:61:63) sts.
Next row K2, skpo, k to last 4 sts, k2 tog, k2.
Next row P to end.
Rep the last 2 rows 5(6:7:8:9) times more. 39(41:41:43:43) sts.
Cast off 2 sts at beg of next 12 rows.
Cast off.

COLLAR

Join shoulder seams.
With wrong side facing and 3mm (US 2) needles, beg at neck shaping,
pick up and k63(72:81:90:99) sts up left front to shoulder, k across
30(32:34:36:38) sts on back neck holder, pick up and k63(72:81:90:99) sts
down right front to beg of neck shaping.
Beg with a p row, work in st st.
Next 2 rows P to last 60(68:76:84:92) sts, turn, k to last
60(68:76:84:92) sts, turn.
Next 2 rows P to last 56(64:72:80:88) sts, turn, k to last
56(64:72:80:88) sts, turn.
Next 2 rows P to last 52(60:68:76:80) sts, turn, k to last
52(60:68:76:80) sts, turn.
Next 2 rows P to last 48(52:56:64:72) sts, turn, k to last
48(52:56:64:72) sts, turn.
Next 2 rows P to last 44(48:52:60:64) sts, turn, k to last 44(48:52:60:64)
sts, turn.
Next 2 rows P to last 40(44:48:56:60) sts, turn, k to last 40(44:48:56:60)
sts, turn.
Cont in this way, working 4 more sts on every 2 rows until the
foll 2 rows have been worked.
Next 2 rows P to last 4 sts, turn, k to last 4 sts, turn.
Next row P to end.
K 2 rows.
Cast off.

TO MAKE UP

Join side and sleeve seams. Sew in sleeves. Sew on buttons. Catch last
row ends of collar in place.

CHRISTMAS

CHRISTMAS IS AN IMPORTANT SEASON FOR US
IN SCANDINAVIA, WITH PLENTY OF TRADITIONS
TO ENJOY WITH NEW GENERATIONS – AMONG
THEM COOKING AND KNITTING.

DANSA ELK DRESS

SKILL LEVEL IMPROVING

SIZES / MEASUREMENTS

To fit age	1–2	2–3	3–4	4–5	5–6	6–7	years

ACTUAL MEASUREMENTS

Chest	51	56	61	65	70	75	cm
	20	22	24	25½	27½	29½	in
Length to back neck	45	50	55	60	65	70	cm
	17¾	19¾	21¾	23¾	25½	27½	in
Sleeve length	21	24	26	28	31	34	cm
	8¼	9½	10¼	11	12¼	13½	in

MATERIALS

3(4:4:5:5:6) 50g/1¾oz balls of MillaMia Naturally Soft Merino in Putty Grey (121) (M).
2(2:2:3:3:3) balls of Storm (102) (A).
3(3:3:4:4:4) balls of Snow (124) (B).
Pair each of 3mm (US 2) and 3.25mm (US 3) knitting needles.
Circular 3.25mm (US 3) knitting needle.
4 buttons approx 12mm/½in in diameter.

TENSION / GAUGE

25 sts and 34 rows to 10cm/4in square over st st using 3.25mm (US 3) needles.

HINTS AND TIPS

In this dress, as with all Fair Isle knitting, it is really important to not pull too tightly when you are knitting the Fair Isle pattern because otherwise it will cause the dress to pull in at the bottom when in fact it should be flaring.

ABBREVIATIONS

See page 11.

ALTERNATIVE COLOURWAYS

Claret 104 Midnight 101 Snow 124

Scarlet 140 Snow 124 Midnight 101

Plum 162 Claret 104 Snow 124

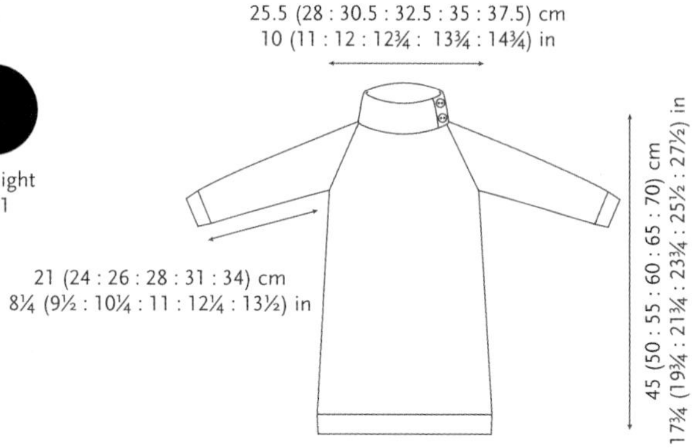

25.5 (28 : 30.5 : 32.5 : 35 : 37.5) cm
10 (11 : 12 : 12¾ : 13¾ : 14¾) in

21 (24 : 26 : 28 : 31 : 34) cm
8¼ (9½ : 10¼ : 11 : 12¼ : 13½) in

45 (50 : 55 : 60 : 65 : 70) cm
17¾ (19¾ : 21¾ : 23¾ : 25½ : 27½) in

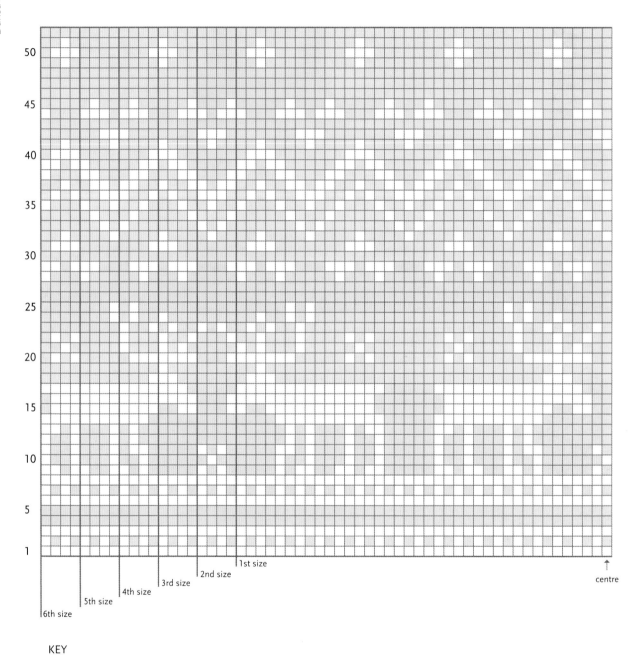

50
45
40
35
30
25
20
15
10
5
1

1st size
2nd size
3rd size
4th size
5th size
6th size
centre

KEY
M – Putty Grey (121)
C – Snow (124)

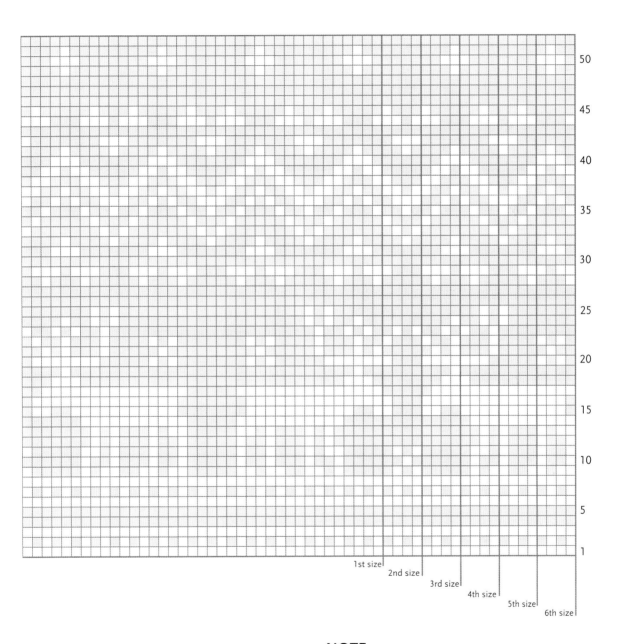

50

45

40

35

30

25

20

15

10

5

1

1st size
2nd size
3rd size
4th size
5th size
6th size

NOTE
The chart has been divided in two sections where the pages of the book join. Work across the stitches of both sections for each row when working the chart.

BACK

With 3mm (US 2) needles and A cast on 74(82:90:98:106:114) sts.

1st rib row P3, [k4, p4] to last 7 sts, k4, p3.

2nd rib row P to end.

Rep the last 2 rows 6(6:7:7:8:8) times more.

Change to 3.25mm (US 3) needles and M.

Beg with a k row, cont in st st.

Work 6(6:8:8:10:10) rows, inc one st at centre of last row.

Work 52 rows in patt from Chart, working between lines indicated for correct size and dec one st at centre of last row.

Dec row K4, skpo, k to last 6 sts, k2 tog, k4.

Work 9 rows.

Rep the last 10 rows 2(3:4:5:6:7) times more, and then the dec row again. 66(72:78:84:90:96) sts.

Cont in st st until back measures 33(37:41:45:49:53)cm/ 13(14½:16¼:17¾:19¼:21)in from cast on edge, ending with a p row.

Shape raglan armholes

Cast off 4 sts at beg of next 2 rows. 58(64:70:76:82:88) sts.

Next row K1, skpo, k to last 3 sts, k2 tog, k1.

Next row P to end.

Next row K to end.

Next row P to end.

Rep the last 4 rows 4 times more. 48(54:60:66:72:78) sts **.

Next row K1, skpo, k to last 3 sts, k2 tog, k1.

Next row P to end.

Rep the last 2 rows 8(10:12:14:16:18) times more. 30(32:34:36:38:40) sts.

Leave these sts on a holder.

FRONT

Work as given for back to ✼✼.

Next row K1, skpo, k to last 3 sts, k2 tog, k1.

Next row P to end.

Rep the last 2 rows 1(3:5:7:9:11) times more. 44(46:48:50:52:54) sts.

Shape front neck

Next row K1, skpo, k11, k2 tog, k1, turn and work on these sts for first side of front neck.

Next row P to end.

Next row K1, skpo, k to last 3 sts, k2 tog, k1.

Next row P to end.

Rep the last 2 rows 4 times more. 5 sts.

Next row K1, sl 1, k2 tog, psso, k1.

Next row P to end.

Leave these 3 sts on a holder.

With right side facing, slip centre 10(12:14:16:18:20) sts onto a holder, rejoin yarn to rem sts, k1, skpo, k11, k2 tog, k1.

Next row P to end.

Next row K1, skpo, k to last 3 sts, k2 tog, k1.

Next row P to end.

Rep the last 2 rows 4 times more. 5 sts.

Next row K1, k3 tog, k1.

Next row P to end.

Leave these 3 sts on a holder.

SLEEVES

With 3mm (US 2) needles and A cast on 42(42:47:47:52:52) sts.

1st rib row P2, [k3, p2] to end.

2nd rib row K2, [p3, k2] to end.

Rep the last 2 rows 5(5:6:6:7:7) times more, inc −(3:1:4:2:5) sts evenly across last row. 42(45:48:51:54:57) sts.

Change to 3.25mm (US 3) needles and B.

Beg with a k row, cont in st st.

Work 2 rows.

Inc row K3, m1, k to last 3 sts, m1, k3.

Work 5 rows.

Rep the last 6 rows 4(5:6:7:8:9) times more, and then the inc row again. 54(59:64:69:74:79) sts.

Cont straight until sleeve measures 21(24:26:28:31:34)cm/8¼(9½:10¼: 11:12¼:13½)in from cast on edge, ending with a p row.

Shape sleeve top
Cast off 4 sts at beg of next 2 rows. 46(51:56:61:66:71) sts.
Next row K2, skpo, k to last 4 sts, k2 tog, k2.
Next row P to end.
Next row K to end.
Next row P to end.
Rep the last 4 rows 2(3:4:5:6:7) times more. 40(43:46:49:52:55) sts.
Next row K2, skpo, k to last 4 sts, k2 tog, k2.
Next row P to end.
Rep the last 2 rows until 14(17:20:23:26:29) sts rem, ending with a
p row.
Leave these sts on a holder.

COLLAR

With 3.25mm (US 3) circular needle and A, k3 from left front holder,
pick up and k14 sts down left side of front neck, k10(12:14:16:18:20) sts
from centre front holder, pick up and k13 sts up right side of front
neck, k2 from holder, k last st on holder tog with first st on right sleeve,
k12(15:18:21:24:27), k last st tog with first st on back, k28(30:32:34:36:38),
k last st on back tog with first st on left sleeve, k13(16:19:22:25:28) from
left sleeve, turn, cast on 6 sts for buttonband. 104(114:124:134:144:154) sts.
Work backwards and forwards in rows.
1st row (right side of collar) K6, [p2, k3] to last 8 sts, p2, k6.
2nd row K1, p5, [k2, p3] to last 8 sts, k2, p5, k1.
These 2 rows form the rib.
Work a further 4 rows.
Buttonhole row Rib to last 6 sts, k2 tog, y2rn, skpo, k2.
Rib 9(9:9:11:11:11) rows.
Rep the last 10(10:10:12:12:12) rows twice more, and then the buttonhole
row again.
Rib 5 rows.
Cast off loosely in rib.

TO MAKE UP

Join raglan seams. Join side and sleeve seams. Catch down cast on edge
of buttonband at neck edge. Sew on buttons.

A SMART BOY

SO SWEET ON, THIS IS THE PERFECT ITEM TO LIVEN UP THE OUTFIT FOR ANY
LITTLE BOYS IN YOUR LIFE OVER THE FESTIVE SEASON.

LASSE TANK TOP

SKILL LEVEL IMPROVING

SIZES / MEASUREMENTS

To fit age	1–2	3–4	5–6	7–8	years

ACTUAL MEASUREMENTS

Chest	52	58	61	68	cm
	20½	23	24	26¾	in

Length to shoulder	30	34	39	45	cm
	12	13½	15½	17¾	in

MATERIALS

2(2:3:3) 50g/1¾oz balls of MillaMia Naturally Soft Merino in Putty Grey (121) (M).
1(1:2:2) balls of Snow (124) (C).
Pair each of 3mm (US 2) and 3.25mm (US 3) knitting needles.

TENSION / GAUGE

25 sts and 34 rows to 10cm/4in square over st st using 3.25mm (US 3) needles.

HINTS AND TIPS

As a tank top there is a limited amount of knitting, making it ideal if you are not that experienced with the Fair Isle technique. When doing colourwork make sure you do not pull the yarn you are carrying behind the knitting too tight, as this will cause the fabric to pucker.

ABBREVIATIONS

See page 11.

NOTE

When working from Chart, right side rows are read from right to left and wrong side rows from left to right.

26 (29 : 30.5 : 34) cm
10¼ (11½ : 12 : 13½) in

30 (34 : 39 : 45) cm
12 (13½ : 15½ : 17¾) in

ALTERNATIVE COLOURWAYS

Midnight Snow
101   124

Fawn Snow
160   124

Scarlet Snow
140   124

BACK

With 3mm (US 2) needles and M cast on 66(74:78:86) sts.
1st rib row K2, [p2, k2] to end.
2nd rib row P2, [k2, p2] to end.
Rep the last 2 rows 3(4:4:5) times more, inc one st evenly across last row. 67(75:79:87) sts.
Join on C.
Change to 3.25mm (US 3) needles.
Work from Chart
1st row K2 sts before patt rep, [work across 4 st patt rep] 16(18:19:21) times, k1 st after patt rep.
2nd row P1 st before patt rep, [work across 4 st patt rep] 16(18:19:21) times, p2 sts after patt rep.
These 2 rows set the Chart.
Cont in patt until back measures 18(21:25:30)cm/7(8¼:10:12)in from cast on edge, ending with a p row.
Shape armholes
Cast off 5 sts at beg of next 2 rows. 57(65:69:77) sts **.
Next row Skpo, patt to last 2 sts, k2 tog.
Next row Patt to end.
Rep the last 2 rows 3(5:5:7) times more. 49(53:57:61) sts.
Cont in st st until back measures 30(34:39:45)cm/12(13½:15½:17¾)in from cast on edge, ending with a wrong side row.
Shape shoulders
Cast off 10(11:12:13) sts at beg of next 2 rows. 29(31:33:35) sts.
Cast off.

FRONT

Work as given for back to **.
Shape front neck
Next row Skpo, patt 24(28:30:34), k2 tog, turn and work on these sts for first side of front neck.
Next row Patt to end.
Next row Skpo, patt to last 2 sts, k2 tog.
Next row Patt to end.
Rep the last 2 rows 3(4:5:6) times more. 18(20:20:22) sts.
Keeping armhole edge straight, cont to dec at neck edge on 4 foll alt rows then every foll 4th row until 10(11:12:13) sts rem.
Cont straight until front measures same as back to shoulder, ending at armhole edge.
Shape shoulder
Cast off.
With right side facing, slip centre st onto a safety pin, join on yarn to rem sts, skpo, patt to last 2 sts, k2 tog.
Next row Patt to end.
Next row Skpo, patt to last 2 sts, k2 tog.

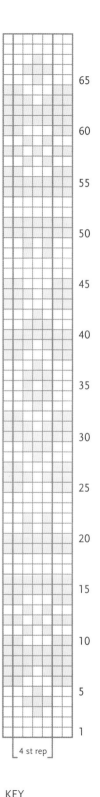

4 st rep

KEY

M – Putty Grey (121
C – Snow (124)

Next row Patt to end.

Rep the last 2 rows 3(4:5:6) times more. 18(20:20:22) sts.

Keeping armhole edge straight, cont to dec at neck edge on 4 foll alt rows then every foll 4th row until 10(11:12:13) sts rem.

Cont straight until front measures same as back to shoulder, ending at armhole edge.

Shape shoulder

Cast off.

NECKBAND

Join right shoulder seam.

With right side facing, using 3mm (US 2) needles and M, pick up and k38(42:44:48) sts evenly down left side of front neck, k1 from safety pin, pick up and k38(40:44:46) sts evenly up right side of front neck, 32(34:36:38) sts from back neck. 109(117:125:133) sts.

3rd and 4th sizes only

1st row [P2, k2] –(–:20:21) times, p1, [k2, p2] to end.

1st and 2nd sizes only

1st row [K2, p2] 17(18:–:–) times, k2, p1, k2, [p2, k2] to end.

All sizes

This row sets the rib.

2nd row Rib 37(41:43:47), s2kpo, rib to end.

3rd row Rib to end.

4th row Rib 36(40:42:46), s2kpo, rib to end.

5th row Rib to end.

2nd, 3rd and 4th sizes only

6th row Rib –(39:41:45), s2kpo, rib to end.

7th row Rib to end.

8th row Rib –(38:40:44), s2kpo, rib to end.

9th row Rib to end.

All sizes

Cast off in rib, dec on this row as before.

Join left shoulder seam and neckband.

ARMBANDS

With right side facing, using 3mm (US 2) needles and M, pick up and k86(94:98:102) sts evenly around armhole edge.

1st row P2, [k2, p2] to end.

2nd row K2, [p2, k2] to end.

These 2 rows form the rib.

Work a further 5(5:7:7) rows.

Cast off in rib.

TO MAKE UP

Join side and armband seams.

MINI CHRISTMAS STOCKINGS

SKILL LEVEL IMPROVING

SIZES / MEASUREMENTS
Approx 11cm/4¼in long by 7cm/2¾in wide at the top.

MATERIALS
One 50g/1¾oz ball of MillaMia Naturally Soft merino in each of Snow (124) (M) and Scarlet (140) (C).
Pair each of 2.75mm (US 2) and 3.25mm (US 3) knitting needles.

TENSION / GAUGE
25 sts and 34 rows to 10cm/4in square over st st using 3.25mm (US 3) needles.

HINTS AND TIPS
These five little stockings are small enough to be used as tree decorations yet still stylish enough to be hung on their own on a mantelpiece or similar. Experiment with modern colour combinations to tone these to your own design scheme for Christmas. These stockings are knitted flat and then seamed to finish.

ABBREVIATIONS
See page 11.

ALTERNATIVE COLOURWAYS

Putty Grey 121   Storm 102   Moss 103   Snow 124

Midnight 101   Fuchsia 143   Fawn 160   Snow 124

7 cm / 2¾ in

11 cm / 4¼ in

10 cm / 4 in

HEART STOCKING

With 2.75mm (US 2) needles and C cast on 68 sts.
K 1 row.
Next row Cast off 30 sts, k to end. 38 sts.
K 7 rows.
Join on M.
Change to 3.25mm (US 3) needles.
Beg with a k row, cont in st st.
1st row Using M, k to end.
2nd row Using M, p to end.
3rd row K [1M, 1C] to end.
4th row P [1M, 1C] to end.
5th and 6th rows As 1st and 2nd rows.
7th row K5M, work across 1st row of Chart, k10M,
work across 1st row of Chart, k5M.
8th row P5M, work across 2nd row of Chart, p10M,
work across 2nd row of Chart, p5M.
These 2 rows set the Chart.
9th to 15th rows Work in patt to end of Chart.
16th row Using M, p to end.
17th row Using M, k to end.
18th row P [1M, 1C] to end.
19th row K [1M, 1C] to end.
Work 3 rows in M.
✳✳ **Next row** K10, skpo, k14, k2 tog, k10. 36 sts.
Cont in C only.
Shape heel
Next row P9, turn.
Work 9 rows in st st on these 9 sts only.
Dec row P3, p2 tog, p1, turn.
Next row Sl 1, k4.
Dec row P4, p2 tog, p1, turn.
Next row Sl 1, k5.
Dec row P5, p2 tog.
Break off C and leave rem 6 sts on a holder.
With wrong side facing, slip next 18 sts onto a holder,
join on C to rem sts, p to end.
Work 8 rows in st st on these 9 sts.

Dec row K3, k2 tog tbl, k1, turn.
Next row Sl 1, p4.
Dec row K4, k2 tog tbl, k1, turn.
Next row Sl 1, p5.
Dec row K5, k2 tog tbl, turn.
Next row Sl 1, p5.
Cont in M only.
Shape instep
Next row K6, pick up and k8 sts evenly along inside
edge of heel, k18 sts from holder, pick up and k8 sts
along inside edge of heel, k6 sts from holder. 46 sts.
P 1 row.
Dec row K12, k2 tog, k18, k2 tog tbl, k12.
P 1 row.
Dec row K11, k2 tog, k18, k2 tog tbl, k11.
P 1 row.
Dec row K10, k2 tog, k18, k2 tog tbl, k10.
P 1 row.
Dec row K9, k2 tog, k18, k2 tog tbl, k9.
Work 13 rows straight.
Cont in C only.
Shape toe
Dec row K1, [k2 tog tbl, k7] 4 times, k1.
P 1 row.
Dec row K1, [k2 tog tbl, k6] 4 times, k1.
P 1 row.
Dec row K1, [k2 tog tbl, k5] 4 times, k1.
P 1 row.
Dec row K1, [k2 tog tbl, k4] 4 times, k1.
P 1 row.
Dec row K1, [k2 tog tbl, k3] 4 times, k1.
P 1 row.
Dec row K1, [k2 tog tbl, k2] 4 times, k1.
Dec row [P2 tog tbl] 7 times.
Break off yarn, thread through rem sts, pull up
and secure.
Join seam and sew loop in place ✳✳.

HEART MOTIF CHART

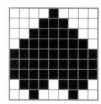

KEY
☐ M – Snow (124)
■ C – Scarlet (140)

NOTE
The motif is deliberately upside
down as these stockings are worked
from the top down.

REINDEER STOCKING

With 2.75mm (US 2) needles and C cast on 68 sts.
K 1 row.
Next row Cast off 30 sts, k to end. 38 sts.
K 7 rows.
Join on M.
Change to 3.25mm (US 3) needles.
Beg with a k row, cont in st st.
1st row Using M, k to end.
2nd row Using M, p to end.
3rd row K [1M, 1C] to end.
4th row Using M, p to end.
5th row K4M, work across 1st row of Chart, k8M,
work across 1st row of Chart, k4M.
6th row P4M, work across 2nd row of Chart, p8M,
work across 2nd row of Chart, p4M.
These 2 rows set the Chart.
7th to 17th rows Work in patt to end of Chart.
18th row Using M, p to end.
19th row K [1M, 1C] to end.
Work 3 rows in M.
Work as given for Heart Stocking from ** to **.

LETTER MOTIF STOCKING

With 2.75mm (US 2) needles and C cast on 68 sts.
K 1 row.
Next row Cast off 30 sts, k to end. 38 sts.
K 7 rows.
Join on M.
Change to 3.25mm (US 3) needles.
Beg with a k row, cont in st st.
1st row Using M, k to end.
2nd row Using M, p to end.
3rd row K2M, [1C, 3M] to end.
4th row P2M, [1C, 1M] to end.
5th row As 3rd row.
6th row Using M, p to end.
7th row Using M, k to end.
8th row P4M, work across 1st row of Chart, p6M,
work across 1st row of Chart, p4M.
9th row K4M, work across 2nd row of Chart, k6M,
work across 2nd row of Chart, p4M.
These 2 rows set the Chart.
10th to 16th rows Work in patt to end of Chart.
17th row Using M, k to end.
18th row Using M, p to end.
19th to 21st rows As 1st to 3rd rows.
Work 1 row in M.
Work as given for Heart Stocking from ** to **.

REINDEER MOTIF CHART

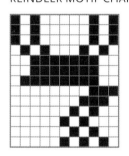

KEY
☐ M – Snow (124)
■ C – Scarlet (140)

NOTE
The motif is deliberately upside
down as these stockings are worked
from the top down.

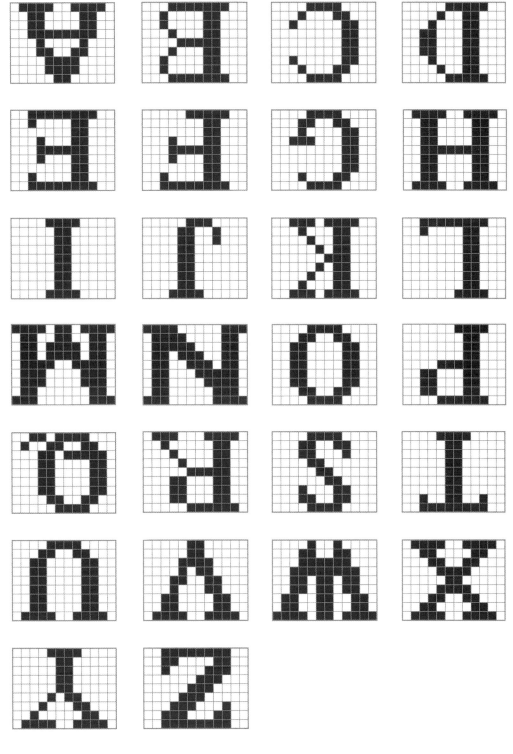

KEY
☐ M – Snow (124)
■ C – Scarlet (140)

NOTE
The motifs are deliberately upside down as these stockings
are worked from the top down.

SNOWFLAKE STOCKING

With 2.75mm (US 2) needles and C cast on 68 sts.

K 1 row.

Next row Cast off 30 sts, k to end. 38 sts.

K 7 rows.

Join on M.

Change to 3.25mm (US 3) needles.

Beg with a k row, cont in st st.

1st row Using M, k to end.

2nd row Using M, p to end.

3rd row K3M, work across 1st row of Chart, k2M, work across 1st row of Chart, k3M.

4th row P3M, work across 2nd row of Chart, p2M, work across 2nd row of Chart, p3M.

These 2 rows set the Chart.

5th to 19th rows Work in patt to end of Chart.

Work 3 rows in M.

Work as given for Heart Stocking from ** to **.

FAIR ISLE STOCKING

With 2.75mm (US 2) needles and C cast on 73 sts.

K 1 row.

Next row Cast off 30 sts, k to end. 43 sts.

K 7 rows.

Join on M.

Change to 3.25mm (US 3) needles.

Beg with a k row, cont in st st and patt from Fair Isle Chart.

1st row Patt 1 st before patt rep, [work across 8 st patt rep] 5 times, patt 2 sts after patt rep.

2nd row Patt 2 sts before patt rep, [work across 8 st patt rep] 5 times, patt 1 st after patt rep.

These 2 rows set the Chart.

Cont in patt for a further 24 rows, ending with a wrong side row.

Cut yarns.

With wrong side facing, slip sts onto other needle.

Cont in C only.

SNOWFLAKE MOTIF CHART

FAIR ISLE MOTIF CHART

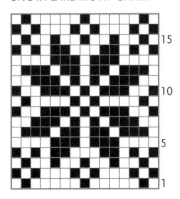

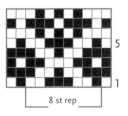

8 st rep

KEY

☐ M – Snow (124)
■ C – Scarlet (140)

Shape heel

Next row P9, turn.

Work 9 rows in st st on these 9 sts only.

Dec row P3, p2 tog, p1, turn.

Next row Sl 1, k4.

Dec row P4, p2 tog, p1, turn.

Next row Sl 1, k5.

Dec row P5, p2 tog.

Break off C and leave rem 6 sts on a holder.

With wrong side facing, slip next 25 sts onto a holder, join on C to rem sts, p to end.

Work 8 rows in st st on these 9 sts.

Dec row K3, k2 tog tbl, k1, turn.

Next row Sl 1, p4.

Dec row K4, k2 tog tbl, k1, turn.

Next row Sl 1, p5.

Dec row K5, k2 tog tbl, turn.

Next row Sl 1, p5.

Shape instep

Next row Using C, k6, pick up and k8 sts evenly along inside edge of heel, patt 25 sts from holder, using C, pick up and k8 sts along inside edge of heel and k6 sts from holder. 53 sts.

Next row P14C, patt 25, p14C.

Dec row Using C, k12, k2 tog, patt 25, using C, k2 tog tbl, k12.

Next row P13C, patt 25, p13C.

Dec row Using C, k11, k2 tog, patt 25, using C, k2 tog tbl, k11.

Next row P12C, patt 25, p12C.

Dec row Using C, k10, k2 tog, patt 25, using C, k2 tog tbl, k10.

Next row P11C, patt 25, p11C.

Dec row Using C, k9, k2 tog, patt 25, using C, k2 tog tbl, k9.

Next row P10C, patt 25, p10C.

Dec row Using C, k8, k2 tog, patt 25, using C, k2 tog tbl, k8. 43 sts

Work 13 rows straight as set.

Cont in C only.

Shape toe

Dec row K2, [k2 tog tbl, k6] 5 times, k1.

P 1 row.

Dec row K2, [k2 tog tbl, k5] 5 times, k1.

P 1 row.

Dec row K2, [k2 tog tbl, k4] 5 times, k1.

P 1 row.

Dec row K2, [k2 tog tbl, k3] 5 times, k1.

P 1 row.

Dec row K2, [k2 tog tbl, k2] 5 times, k1.

Dec row [P2 tog tbl] 9 times.

Break off yarn, thread through rem sts, pull up and secure.

Join seam and sew loop in place.

BOKSTAV GIFT TAGS

SKILL LEVEL BEGINNER / IMPROVING

SIZES / MEASUREMENTS
Approx 5.5cm/2¼in high; width varies depending on letter.

MATERIALS
Small amount of MillaMia Naturally Soft Merino in each of
Midnight (101) (M) and Snow (124) (C).
Pair of 3.25mm (US 3) knitting needles.

TENSION / GAUGE
25 sts and 34 rows to 10cm/4in square over patt using
3.25mm (US 3) needles.

HINTS AND TIPS
These double-sided gift tags are the perfect addition to any gift wrap.
Save them and reuse them year on year for your family members. The
letters are Swiss darned onto the gift tags because we think this gives
the most solid look, but if you prefer you could of course work them
into the fabric of the knitting using the intarsia method. Once finished,
press flat with an iron for a neat, precise finish.

ABBREVIATIONS
See page 11.

ALTERNATIVE COLOURWAYS

Scarlet Snow
140   124

Fuchsia Peacock
143   144

Storm Putty
102   Grey
       121

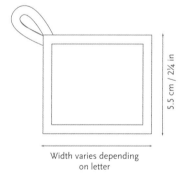

5.5 cm / 2¼ in

Width varies depending
on letter

BACK AND FRONT (Alike)

For letters with an even number of sts

With 3.25mm (US 3) needles and M cast on number of sts in letter
+ 4 + 6 sts.

1st row [K1, p1] to end.

2nd row [P1, k1] to end.

Rep the last 2 rows once more.

For letters with an odd number of sts

With 3.25mm (US 3) needles and M cast on number of sts in letter
+ 4 + 6 sts.

Moss st row K1, [p1, k1] to end.

Rep this row 3 times more.

For all letters

Work in st st with moss st border.

1st row Using M moss st 3, using C k to last 3 sts, using M moss st 3.

2nd row Using M moss st 3, using C p to last 3 sts, using M moss st 3.

Rep the last 2 rows 5 times more, and then the 1st row again.

Cont in M only.

Next row Moss st 3, p to last 3 sts, moss st 3.

Work 3 rows moss st.

Back only

Cast off in moss st.

Front only

Cast on 20 sts for loop, cast off 20 sts knitwise, then cast off rem sts in
moss st.

TO MAKE UP

Using M, work from alphabet letter Charts and Swiss darn letters within
2 st/2 row border of C. Leaving end of loop free, join sides. Sew end of
loop to beg of loop.

KEY
- ■ M – Midnight (101)
- □ C – Snow (124)

PEPPARKAKOR

THIS IS A FAMILY RECIPE PASSED DOWN FROM OUR FATHER'S AUNTS (WHO IN TURN WERE TAUGHT IT BY THEIR AUNTS). WE BAKE IT EVERY YEAR WITH OUR GRANDMOTHER AND MOTHER. PREPARE THE DOUGH THE DAY BEFORE YOU WANT TO BAKE THE GINGERBREAD FOR OPTIMAL RESULTS.

DELICIOUS AND HANDMADE

HALF THE CHARM OF THESE IS AN IMPERFECT FINISH. LET THE KIDS ENJOY ICING.

PEPPARKAKOR

MAKES OVER 100 GINGERBREAD DEPENDING ON THE SIZE

INGREDIENTS
500g/1lb 2oz golden syrup
400g/14oz caster sugar
400g/14oz unsalted butter, cubed
1 tbsp ground cinnamon
1 tbsp ground cloves
1½ tsp ground ginger
1kg/2lb 3oz plain flour (plus extra for rolling out)
2 large egg yolks
2 tsp bicarbonate of soda, blended with a little water
to make a thick paste

For the icing
200g/7oz icing sugar, sifted
2 tbsp water

DOUGH
Put the syrup and sugar in a saucepan, stir to combine, and cook over a medium heat until bubbling and golden brown. Remove the pan from the heat. Gradually add the butter in small pieces, stirring to mix until melted and combined. Pour the mixture into a large bowl. Mix in the spices followed by a small amount of the flour, the egg yolks and the bicarbonate of soda paste. Stir well, gradually adding the remaining flour until the mixture forms a smooth, wet dough. Cover with cling film and leave to rest in the fridge to firm up for at least 8 hours, or overnight.

BAKING
Line a large baking sheet with baking paper. Preheat the oven to 175°C/350°F/gas mark 4. Working in batches, roll out the dough on a floured surface as thinly as you can (ideally about 1–2mm) for gingerbread with a snap. Cut out desired shapes, then transfer to the lined baking sheet using a palette knife, spacing them well apart. Bake for 6–8 minutes until light brown. Transfer to wire racks and leave to cool completely.

ICING
Put the icing sugar in a bowl and gradually stir in enough of the water to form a smooth paste. Using a piping bag, decorate gingerbread with designs of your choice. Leave to set in a cool, dry place. Store gingerbread in an airtight container for up to 20 days.

NAMN CHRISTMAS STOCKING

SKILL LEVEL IMPROVING

SIZES / MEASUREMENTS
Approx 30cm/12in long by 16cm/6¼in wide at the top.

MATERIALS
Two 50g/1¾oz balls of MillaMia Naturally Soft Merino in Snow (124) (M).
One ball of Scarlet (140) (C).
Pair each of 3mm (US 2) and 3.25mm (US 3) knitting needles.

TENSION / GAUGE
25 sts and 34 rows to 10cm/4in over st st using 3.25mm (US 3) needles.

HINTS AND TIPS
These stockings are knitted flat and finished by seaming up the back. Try to use mattress stitch for a flawless finish. Have fun making these for everyone important in your life – they will become heirlooms to be treasured.

ABBREVIATIONS
See page 11.

NOTE
When working from Charts, right side rows are k rows and read from right to left, wrong side rows are p rows and read from left to right. When working from Charts 1 and 2, use the Fair Isle method. When working from the alphabet letter Charts, use the intarsia method.

ALTERNATIVE COLOURWAYS

Snow   Moss   Putty   Midnight   Snow   Grass
124   103   Grey   101   124   141
                121

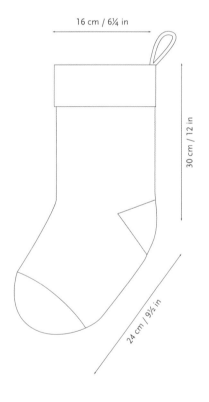

16 cm / 6¼ in

30 cm / 12 in

24 cm / 9½ in

THE PERSONAL TOUCH

CUSTOMISE ONE WITH AN INITIAL FOR EACH OF YOUR FAMILY.

STOCKING

With 3mm (US 2) needles and C cast on 81 sts.
Moss st row K1, [p1, k1] to end.
Cont in moss st until cuff measures 7cm/2¾in
from cast on edge.
Next row P to end, inc one st at centre. 82 sts
Mark each end of last row with a coloured thread.
Break off C.
Join on M.
Beg with a k row, cont in st st until work
measures 7cm/2¾in from coloured threads,
ending with a p row.
Change to 3.25mm (US 3) needles.
Work 6 rows st st.
Work in patt from Chart 1.
7th row [K across 2 st patt rep of 1st row of Chart]
41 times.
8th row [P across 2 st patt rep of 2nd row of
Chart] 41 times.
9th row Using M, k to end.
Work in patt from Chart 2.
10th row P first st of Chart, [p across 4 st patt rep
of 1st row of Chart] 20 times, p last st of Chart.
11th row K first st of Chart, [k across 4 st patt rep
of 2nd row of Chart] 20 times, k last st of Chart.
12th row P first st of Chart, [p across 4 st patt rep
of 3rd row of Chart] 20 times, p last st of Chart.
Using M, work 3 rows st st.
Work in patt from your chosen alphabet
letter Chart.
Letters 'A', 'V' and 'X' only
16th row P10M, p across 1st row of Chart, p16M,
p across 1st row of Chart, p10M.
17th row K10M, k across 2nd row of Chart, k16M,
k across 2nd row of Chart, k10M.
Letters 'B', 'C', 'F' and 'K' only
16th row P13M, p across 1st row of Chart, p22M,
p across 1st row of Chart, p13M.
17th row K13M, k across 2nd row of Chart, k22M,
k across 2nd row of Chart, k13M.
Letters 'D', 'H', 'N' and 'O' only
16th row P11M, p across 1st row of Chart, p20M,
p across 1st row of Chart, p11M.
17th row K11M, k across 2nd row of Chart, k20M,
k across 2nd row of Chart, k11M.
Letters 'E', 'R', 'T' and 'Z' only
16th row P12M, p across 1st row of Chart, p22M,
p across 1st row of Chart, p12M.
17th row K12M, k across 2nd row of Chart, k22M,
k across 2nd row of Chart, k12M.

Letter 'G' only
16th row P12M, p across 1st row of Chart,
p20M, p across 1st row of Chart, p12M.
17th row K12M, k across 2nd row of Chart,
k20M, k across 2nd row of Chart, k12M.
Letter 'I' only
16th row P16M, p across 1st row of Chart,
p28M, p across 1st row of Chart, p16M.
17th row K16M, k across 2nd row of Chart,
k28M, k across 2nd row of Chart, k16M.
Letters 'J' and 'S' only
16th row P15M, p across 1st row of Chart,
p26M, p across 1st row of Chart, p15M.
17th row K15M, k across 2nd row of Chart,
k26M, k across 2nd row of Chart, k15M.
Letters 'L' and 'P' only
16th row P14M, p across 1st row of Chart,
p24M, p across 1st row of Chart, p14M.
17th row K14M, k across 2nd row of Chart,
k24M, k across 2nd row of Chart, k14M.
Letters 'M', 'Q', 'U' and 'Y' only
16th row P9M, p across 1st row of Chart, p22M,
p across 1st row of Chart, p9M.
17th row K9M, k across 2nd row of Chart, k22M,
k across 2nd row of Chart, k9M.
Letter 'W' only
16th row P8M, p across 1st row of Chart, p12M,
p across 1st row of Chart, p8M.
17th row K8M, k across 2nd row of Chart, k12M,
k across 2nd row of Chart, k8M.
All Letters
These 2 rows set the Chart.
18th to 35th rows Work in patt to end of Chart.
Using M, work 3 rows st st.
Work in patt from Chart 2.
39th row K first st of Chart, [k across 4 st patt rep
of 1st row of Chart] 20 times, k last st of Chart.
40th row P first st of Chart, [p across 4 st patt
rep of 2nd row of Chart] 20 times, p last st
of Chart.

CHART 1

2 st
rep

CHART 2

4 st rep

KEY

☐ M – Snow (124)
■ C – Scarlet (140)

NOTE
The motifs are deliberately upside down as these
stockings are worked from the top down.

41st row K first st of Chart, [k across 4 st patt rep of 3rd row of Chart] 20 times, k last st of Chart.
42nd row Using M, p to end.
Work in patt from Chart 1.
43rd row [K across 2 st patt rep of 1st row of Chart] 41 times.
44th row [P across 2 st patt rep of 2nd row of Chart] 41 times.
Cont in M until work measures 24cm/9½in from coloured threads, ending with a k row.
Cont in C only.
Shape heel
Next row P21, turn.
Work 21 rows in st st on these 21 sts only.
Dec row P4, p2 tog, p1, turn.
Next row Sl 1, k5.
Dec row P6, p2 tog, p1, turn.
Next row Sl 1, k7.
Dec row P8, p2 tog, p1, turn.
Next row Sl 1, k9.
Dec row P10, p2 tog, p1, turn.
Next row Sl 1, k11.
Dec row P12, p2 tog, p1, turn.
Next row Sl 1, k13.
Dec row P14, p2 tog.
Break off C and leave rem 15 sts on a holder.
With wrong side facing, slip next 40 sts onto a holder, join on C to rem sts, p to end.
Work 22 rows in st st on these 21 sts.
Dec row K4, skpo, k1, turn.
Next row Sl 1, p5.
Dec row K6, skpo, k1, turn.
Next row Sl 1, p7.
Dec row K8, skpo, k1, turn.
Next row Sl 1, p9.
Dec row K10, skpo, k1, turn.
Next row Sl 1, p11.
Dec row K12, skpo, k1, turn.
Next row Sl 1, p13.
Dec row K14, skpo, turn.
Next row Sl 1, p14.
Cont in M only.
Shape instep
Next row K15, pick up and k15 sts evenly along inside edge of heel, k40 sts from holder, pick up and k15 sts along inside edge of heel, k15 sts from holder. 100 sts.
P 1 row.
Dec row K28, k2 tog, k40, skpo, k28.

P 1 row.
Dec row K27, k2 tog, k40, skpo, k27.
P 1 row.
Dec row K26, k2 tog, k40, skpo, k26.
P 1 row.
Cont to dec one st either side of the centre 40 sts on next and 5 foll alt rows. 82 sts.
Work 31 rows st st.
Change to C.
Shape toe
Dec row K5, skpo, k28, k2 tog, k8, skpo, k28, k2 tog, k5.
P 1 row.
Dec row K5, skpo, k26, k2 tog, k8, skpo, k26, k2 tog, k5.
P 1 row.
Dec row K5, skpo, k24, k2 tog, k8, skpo, k24, k2 tog, k5.
P 1 row.
Dec row K5, skpo, k22, k2 tog, k8, skpo, k22, k2 tog, k5.
P 1 row.
Dec row K5, skpo, k20, k2 tog, k8, skpo, k20, k2 tog, k5.
P 1 row.
Dec row K5, skpo, k18, k2 tog, k8, skpo, k18, k2 tog, k5. 58 sts.
P 1 row.
Next row Cast off 2 sts, then k26, turn.
Cast off 2 sts at beg of next 7 rows. 13 sts.
Cast off.
With right side facing, rejoin yarn to rem sts, cast off 2 sts, k to end.
Cast off 2 sts at beg of next 7 rows. 13 sts.
Cast off.

LOOP
With 3mm (US 2) needles and C cast on 40 sts.
K 1 row.
Cast off.

TO MAKE UP
Join seam, reversing seam for cuff. Fold cuff to right side. Fold loop in half and attach to back of stocking.

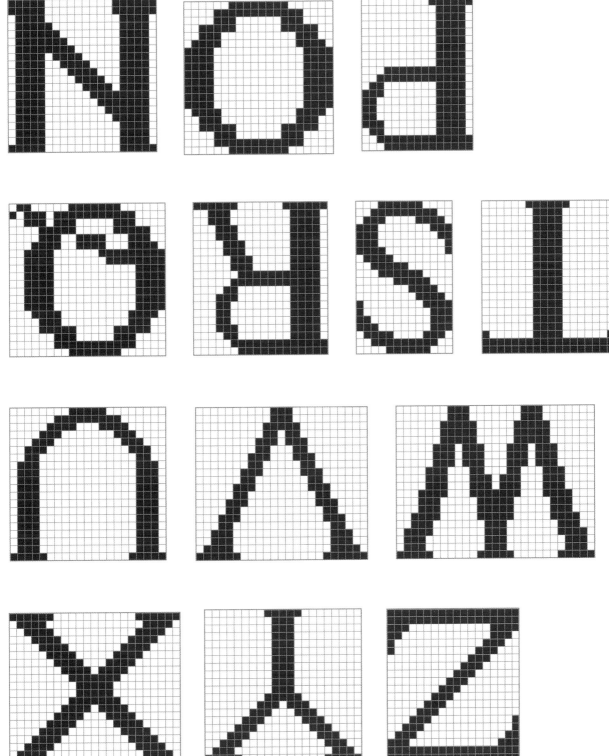

KEY
☐ M – Snow (124)
■ C – Scarlet (140)

NOTE
The motifs are deliberately upside down as these
stockings are worked from the top down.

CELEBRATE

WHEN IT COMES TO THE NEW YEAR — OR FOR
ANY EXCUSE — WE LIKE TO CELEBRATE. MAKE SURE
YOUR HOME LOOKS ITS BEST — YOUR KNITTED
DECORATIONS CAN ADD TO THE GLAMOUR.

THE CUSHION AS ART

THESE CUSHIONS ARE SO STRIKING THAT IT WOULD BE EASY MISTAKE THEM FOR ARTWORK TO BE ADMIRED FROM AFAR.

NORDIC NIGHTSCAPE CUSHION

SKILL LEVEL BEGINNER / IMPROVING

MEASUREMENTS

33cm/13in by 33cm/13in to fit a 35cm/13¾in by 35cm/13¾in cushion pad.

MATERIALS

Four 50g/1¾oz balls of MillaMia Naturally Soft Merino in Midnight (101) (M).
One ball of Snow (124) (C).
Pair of 3.25mm (US 3) knitting needles.

TENSION / GAUGE

25 sts and 34 rows to 10cm/4in square over st st using 3.25mm (US 3) needles.

HINTS AND TIPS

This is a stunning cushion that will quickly become a focal point in your home. We Swiss darn (also known as duplicate stitch) the design onto the cushion after knitting because we feel this gives the best finished result. There are plenty of Swiss darning tutorials on the internet if you are new to this technique. A top tip is to not pull too tight when Swiss darning – by doing a looser stitch you get a more even coverage over the original stitch. See page p156 for more guidance.

ABBREVIATIONS

See page 11.

ALTERNATIVE COLOURWAYS

Scarlet 140 Snow 124

Pitch Black 100 Snow 124

Storm 102 Snow 124

33 cm / 13 in

33 cm / 13 in

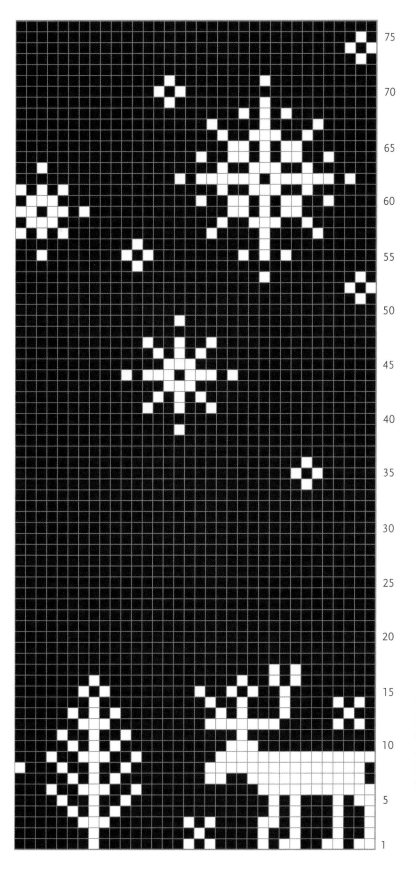

NOTE

The chart has been divided in two sections where the pages of the book join. When Swiss darning the design, work across both sections as if they were a single chart.

KEY

■ M – Midnight (101)
□ C – Snow (124)

BACK AND FRONT (Both alike)

With 3.25mm (US 3) needles and M cast on 85 sts.
Beg with a k row, cont in st st.
Work 10 rows M, 2 rows C, 2 rows M, 1 row C.
On next row use C from other end of ball. This will
save a couple of ends.
16th row P1M, [1C, 1M] to end.
17th row Using C, k to end.
Work 78 rows M, 1 row C.
97th row K1M, [1C, 1M] to end.
98th row Using C, p to end.
Work 2 rows M, 2 rows C, 10 rows M.
Using M, cast off.

TO MAKE UP

Working from Chart and using C, Swiss darn the
Nordic nightscape. With right sides together, sew
back to front along 3 sides. Turn to right side. Insert
cushion pad. Join remaining seam.

FIRST FALL TABLE RUNNER

SKILL LEVEL BEGINNER / IMPROVING

MEASUREMENTS
Approx 32cm/12½in wide by 110cm/43¼in long.

MATERIALS
Five 50g/1¾oz balls of MillaMia Naturally Soft Merino in Storm (102) (M).
One ball of Snow (124) (C).
Pair of 3.25mm (US 3) knitting needles.

TENSION / GAUGE
25 sts and 34 rows to 10cm/4in square over patt using 3.25mm
(US 3) needles.

HINTS AND TIPS
While we give a recommended size for this table runner, you could of
course make it longer or shorter according to your own requirements.
This may affect the amount of yarn required so try to estimate this if you
do change the length. The table runner benefits from being pressed flat
before the motifs are Swiss darned onto it.

ABBREVIATIONS
See page 11.

ALTERNATIVE COLOURWAYS

Fuchsia   Snow
143   124

Seaside   Snow
161   124

Midnight Snow
101   124

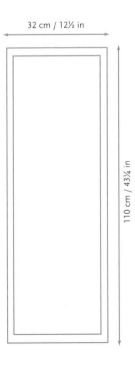

32 cm / 12½ in

110 cm / 43¼ in

TABLE RUNNER

With 3.25mm (US 3) needles and M cast on 75 sts.
Moss st row K1, [p1, k1] to end.
Work a further 8 rows.
Inc row Moss st 12, [m1, moss st 10] 5 times, m1, moss st 13. 81 sts.
Cont in st st with moss st border.
1st row K1, [p1, k1] twice, p1, k to last 6 sts, [p1, k1] 3 times.
2nd row K1, [p1, k1] twice, p to last 5 sts, k1, [p1, k1] twice.
3rd to 142nd rows Rep the 1st and 2nd rows 70 times.
Mark each end of last row with a coloured thread.
143rd to 218th rows Rep the 1st and 2nd rows 38 times.
Mark each end of last row with a coloured thread.
219th to 360th rows Rep the 1st and 2nd rows 71 times.
Dec row Moss st 12, [work 2 tog, moss st 9] 5 times, work 2 tog,
moss st 12. 75 sts.
Work a further 8 rows in moss st.
Cast off in moss st.

TO COMPLETE

Using C, and working inside the moss st border and starting from one
end of the runner, beg at 1st row of Chart, Swiss darn the snowflake
motifs. Markers indicate the position of the final row of the Chart
design. Turn the table runner around, and working inside the moss st
border and starting **at the other end** of the runner, beg at 1st row of
Chart, Swiss darn the snowflake motifs.

KEY
■ M – Storm (102)
□ C – Snow (124)

NOTE

The chart has been divided onto two pages. When Swiss
darning the motifs, follow the section for rows 1–39, then
continue from the section for rows 40–142.

FIRA CHOCOLATE CAKE

ASK ANY SWEDE ABOUT 'KLADD KAKA' (LITERALLY THIS MEANS 'STICKY CAKE') AND THEIR EYES WILL LIGHT UP. THIS SUMPTUOUS, STICKY, BROWNIE-LIKE CAKE IS SO EASY TO MAKE YET SO DELICIOUS THAT IT IS A STAPLE FOR SWEDES FOR BOTH ENTERTAINING AND EVERYDAY USE. AS THIS IS A SWEDISH RECIPE, VOLUME MEASURES ARE GIVEN EVEN FOR DRY MATTER (AS OPPOSED TO WEIGHTS). IF YOU WANT TO MAKE A DOUBLE PORTION USE A 24CM/10IN CAKE TIN AND BAKE FOR 35–40 MINUTES (CHECKING REGULARLY THAT IT DOES NOT GET OVERCOOKED – IT SHOULD BE REALLY STICKY IN THE MIDDLE). SERVE WITH WHIPPED CREAM AND RASPBERRIES FOR A LUXURIOUS FINISH.

3,2,1 CELEBRATE

**A SIMPLE CHOCOLATE CAKE – SERVE WITH PLENTY OF CREAM FOR
A SURE-FIRE SUCCESS.**

FIRA CHOCOLATE CAKE

MAKES ONE 20CM/8IN ROUND CAKE

INGREDIENTS
150g/5oz unsalted butter, melted
2 tbsp desiccated coconut (optional, but adds a wonderful
  secret flavour)
300ml/10fl oz sugar
150ml/5fl oz plain flour
4 tbsp cocoa powder
Pinch of salt
1 tsp vanilla extract (or 2 tsp vanilla sugar)
2 large eggs or 3 small eggs
50–100g/2–4oz white chocolate, roughly chopped

To serve
Icing sugar
Whipped cream or ice cream

PREPARATION
Preheat the oven to 200°C/400°F/gas mark 6. Grease a 20cm/8in round
cake tin with a little melted butter. If using, sprinkle the dessicated
coconut over the base of the tin to form an even layer.

MIXTURE
Mix together the sugar, flour, cocoa powder, salt and vanilla extract in a
large bowl. Then add the eggs and melted butter and mix with a whisk
until well combined. Transfer the mixture into the prepared cake tin.
Add the white chocolate pieces, pressing them down so they are hidden
beneath the surface of the cake mixture.

BAKING
Bake for approx 15–20 minutes until firm to the touch – the cake should
still be wet and sticky in the middle.

SERVING
Leave to cool completely, then dust with icing sugar and serve with
whipped cream (or ice cream if you prefer).

SNOW

WHEN THE SNOW IS FRESH AND IT IS COLD AND
CRISP OUTSIDE, IT IS A JOY. WE FEEL THE SAME
EXCITEMENT EVERY YEAR AS THE SNOW ARRIVES AND
THE CHILDREN (AND ADULTS) ENJOY THEIR FIRST PLAY
WITH SNOWMEN, SNOWBALLS AND SNOW LANTERNS.

MADICKEN CAPE

SKILL LEVEL IMPROVING

SIZES / MEASUREMENTS

To fit bust	82–87	92–97	102–107	112–117	cm
	32–34	36–38	40–42	44–46	in

ACTUAL MEASUREMENTS

Wrist to wrist	102	107	112	117	cm
(including edging)	40	42	44	46	in
Length to shoulder	76	79	81	84	cm
(including edging)	30	31	32	33	in

MATERIALS

19(21:23:25) 50g/1¾oz balls of MillaMia Naturally Soft Merino in Putty Grey (121).
Pair of 3.25mm (US 3) knitting needles.
Circular 3.25mm (US 3) knitting needle.
Cable needle.

TENSION / GAUGE

25 sts and 38 rows to 10cm/4in square over patt using 3.25mm (US 3) needles.

HINTS AND TIPS

This is a big item, lovely and warm and comfortable to wear. The cable detail on the purl garter stitch collar is a key feature and a fun part of the knitting process. In fact as the front and back are quite large pieces of knitting, we found it helpful to alternate between the body pieces and collar every now and then. A circular needle is only used to accommodate the number of stitches – you are still working backwards and forwards in rows rather than in rounds.

ABBREVIATIONS

C8F, cable 8 front – slip next 4 sts onto cable needle and hold at front of work, k4, then k4 from cable needle.
C8B, cable 8 back – slip next 4 sts onto cable needle and hold at back of work, k4, then k4 from cable needle.
See also page 11.

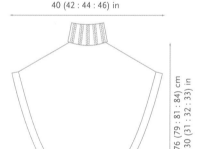

102 (107 : 112 : 117) cm
40 (42 : 44 : 46) in

76 (79 : 81 : 84) cm
30 (31 : 32 : 33) in

ALTERNATIVE COLOURWAYS

Fawn 160

Plum 162

Sable 105

Snow 124

BACK

With 3.25mm (US 3) needles cast on 87(95:103:111) sts.

1st row (right side) K2, [p1, k1] to last st, k1.

2nd row P to end.

These 2 rows set the patt with 2 sts in st st at each end.

Inc row K2, m1, patt to last 2 sts, m1, k2.

Next row P to end.

Changing to circular needle when necessary, and cont to work backwards and forwards in rows, rep the last 2 rows 61 times more. 211(219:227:235) sts.

Inc row K2, m1, patt to last 2 sts, m1, k2.

Next row P to end.

Next row K2, patt to last 2 sts, k2.

Next row P to end.

Rep the last 4 rows 11(13:15:17) times more. 235(247:259:271) sts.

Work 54 rows straight **.

Shape upperarm

Cast off 3 sts at beg of next 44(46:48:50) rows. 103(109:115:121) sts.

Shape shoulders

Cast off 11(12:13:14) sts at beg of next 4 rows. 59(61:63:65) sts.

Cast off.

FRONT

Work as given for back to **.

Cast off 3 sts at beg of next 12(14:16:18) rows. 199(205:211:217) sts.

Shape front neck

1st row Cast off 3 sts, patt until there are 82(84:86:88) sts on the needle, turn and work on these sts for first side of neck.

Next row P to end.

Next row Cast off 3 sts, patt to last 3 sts, k2 tog, k1.

Next row P to end.

Rep the last 2 rows 14 times more. 22(24:26:28) sts.

Shape shoulder

Next row Cast off 11(12:13:14) sts, patt to end.

Work 1 row.

Cast off rem 11(12:13:14) sts.

With right side facing, rejoin yarn to rem sts, cast off centre 29(31:33:35) sts, patt to end.

Next row Cast off 3 sts, p to end.

Next row K1, skpo, patt to end.

Rep the last 2 rows 14 times more.

Next row Cast off 3 sts, p to end. 22(24:26:28) sts.

Next row Patt to end.

Shape shoulder

Next row Cast off 11(12:13:14) sts, patt to end.

Work 1 row.

Cast off rem 11(12:13:14) sts.

EDGING

With 3.25mm (US 3) needles cast on 19 sts.
1st rib row K2, [p1, k1] to last 3 sts, p1, k2.
2nd rib row P2, k1, [p1, k1] to end.
Rep the last 2 rows until edging fits all around outer edges of front and back.
Cast off in rib.

COLLAR

With 3.25mm (US 3) needles cast on 134 sts.
1st row P3, [k8, p4] to last 11 sts, k8, p3.
2nd row P to end.
Rep the last 2 rows 6 times more.
Inc row P3, * k1, [m1, k2] 3 times, m1, k1, p4; rep from * to last 11 sts, k1, [m1, k2] 3 times, m1, k1, p3. 178 sts.
Cont in cable patt with p g-st between.
1st row (right side) P3, [k12, p4] to last 15 sts, k12, p3.
2nd and every foll wrong side row P to end.
3rd row P3, [k4, C8B, p4] to last 15 sts, k4, C8B, p3.
5th row P3, [k12, p4] to last 15 sts, k12, p3.
7th row P3, [C8F, k4, p4] to last 15 sts, C8F, k4, p3.
8th row P to end.
These 8 rows set the cable patt with p g-st between.
Work straight until collar measures 11cm/4¼in from cast on edge, ending with a p row.
Inc row P1, m1, p2, [patt 12, p2, m1, p2] to last 15 sts, patt 12, p3.
Cont in patt working inc sts in p g-st until collar measures 20cm/8in from cast on edge, ending with a p row.
Inc row P4, [patt 12, p2, m1, p3] to last 15 sts, patt 12, p1, m1, p2.
Cont in patt until collar measures 29cm/11½in from cast on edge, ending with a right side row.
Cast off purlwise.

TO MAKE UP

Join shoulder and upperarm seams. Starting at centre of lower back, sew edging around outer edge of cape. Join collar seam. With right side of collar to wrong side of work, and with collar seam to left shoulder, sew cast on edge of collar to neck opening.

LISABET CAPE

SKILL LEVEL IMPROVING

SIZES / MEASUREMENTS

To fit age	2–4	4–6	6–8	8–10	years

ACTUAL MEASUREMENTS

Wrist to wrist	53	63	73	82	cm
(including edging)	21	24¾	28¾	32½	in

Length to shoulder	35	45	56	66	cm
(including edging)	13¾	17¾	22	26	in

MATERIALS

11(12:14:15) 50g/1¾oz balls of MillaMia Naturally Soft Merino in Berry (163).
Pair of 3.25mm (US 3) knitting needles.
Circular 3.25mm (US 3) knitting needle.
Cable needle.

TENSION / GAUGE

25 sts and 38 rows to 10cm/4in square over patt using 3.25mm (US 3) needles.

HINTS AND TIPS

We loved the idea of creating mother and daughter versions of this cape design. Have fun selecting bright, vibrant colours. While a lot of yarn is used, the cape is generously sized and will fit the recipient for many years.

ABBREVIATIONS

C8F, cable 8 front – slip next 4 sts onto cable needle and hold at front of work, k4, then k4 from cable needle.
C8B, cable 8 back – slip next 4 sts onto cable needle and hold at back of work, k4, then k4 from cable needle.
See also page 11.

ALTERNATIVE COLOURWAYS

Fuchsia	Plum	Peacock	Midnight
143	162	144	101

53 (63 : 73 : 82) cm
21 (24¾ : 28¾ : 32½) in

35 (45 : 56 : 66) cm
13¾ (17¾ : 22 : 26) in

BACK

With 3.25mm (US 3) needles cast on 55(61:67:73) sts.

1st row (right side) K2, [p1, k1] to last st, k1.

2nd row P to end.

These 2 rows set the patt with 2 sts in st st at each end.

Inc row K2, m1, patt to last 2 sts, m1, k2.

Next row P2, k to last 2 sts, p2.

Changing to circular needle if necessary and cont to work backwards and forwards in rows, rep the last 2 rows 23(30:37:44) times more. 103(123:143:163) sts.

Inc row K2, m1, patt to last 2 sts, m1, k2.

Next row P2, k to last 2 sts, p2.

Next row K2, patt to last 2 sts, k2.

Next row P2, k to last 2 sts, p2.

Rep the last 4 rows 4(6:8:10) times more. 113(137:161:185) sts.

Work 24(34:44:54) rows straight **.

Shape upperarm

Cast off 2 sts at beg of next 20(28:36:44) rows. 73(81:89:97) sts.

Shape shoulders

Cast off 7(8:9:10) sts at beg of next 4 rows. 45(49:53:57) sts.

Cast off.

FRONT

Work as given for back to **.

Cast off 2 sts at beg of next –(6:12:18) rows. 113(125:137:149) sts.

Shape front neck

1st row Cast off 2 sts, patt until there are 42(47:52:57) sts on the needle, turn and work on these sts for first side of neck.

Next row Patt to end.

Next row Cast off 2 sts, patt to last 3 sts, k2 tog, k1.

Next row Patt to end.

Rep the last 2 rows 8(9:10:11) times more. 15(17:19:21) sts.

Shape shoulder

Next row Cast off 7(8:9:10) sts, patt to last 3 sts, k2 tog, k1.

Work 1 row.

Cast off rem 7(8:9:10) sts.

With right side facing, rejoin yarn to rem sts, cast off centre 25(27:29:31) sts, patt to end.

Next row Cast off 2 sts, patt to end.

Next row K1, skpo, patt to end.

Rep the last 2 rows 9(10:11:12) times more. 14(16:18:20) sts.

Shape shoulder

Next row Cast off 7(8:9:10) sts, patt to end.

Work 1 row.

Cast off rem 7(8:9:10) sts.

EDGING

With 3.25mm (US 3) needles cast on 19 sts.

1st rib row K2, [p1, k1] to last 3 sts, p1, k2.

2nd rib row P2, k1, [p1, k1] to end.

Rep the last 2 rows until edging fits all around outer edges of front and back.

Cast off in rib.

COLLAR

With 3.25mm (US 3) needles cast on 98(110:122:134) sts.

1st row P3, [k8, p4] to last 11 sts, k8, p3.

2nd row P to end.

Rep the last 2 rows 4 times more.

Inc row P3, * k1, [m1, k2] 3 times, m1, k1, p4; rep from * to last 11 sts, k1, [m1, k2] 3 times, m1, k1, p3. 130(146:162:178) sts.

Cont in cable patt with p g-st between.

1st row (right side) P3, [k12, p4] to last 15 sts, k12, p3.

2nd and every foll wrong side row P to end.

3rd row P3, [k4, C8B, p4] to last 15 sts, k4, C8B, p3.

5th row P3, [k12, p4] to last 15 sts, k12, p3.

7th row P3, [C8F, k4, p4] to last 15 sts, C8F, k4, p3.

8th row P to end.

These 8 rows set the cable patt with p g-st between.

Work straight until collar measures 5(7:9:11)cm/2(2¾:3½:4¼)in from cast on edge, ending with a p row.

Inc row P1, m1, p2, [patt 12, p2, m1, p2] to last 15 sts, patt 12, p3.

Cont in patt working inc sts in p g-st until collar measures 11(14:17:20)cm/4¼(5½:6¾:8)in from cast on edge, ending with a p row.

Inc row P4, [patt 12, p2, m1, p3] to last 15 sts, patt 12, p1, m1, p2.

Cont in patt until collar measures 12(16:20:24)cm/4¾(6¼:8:9½)in from cast on edge, ending with a right side row.

Cast off purlwise.

TO MAKE UP

Join shoulder and upperarm seams. Starting at centre of lower back, sew edging around outer edge of cape. Join collar seam. With right side of collar to wrong side of work, and with collar seam to left shoulder, sew cast on edge of collar to neck opening.

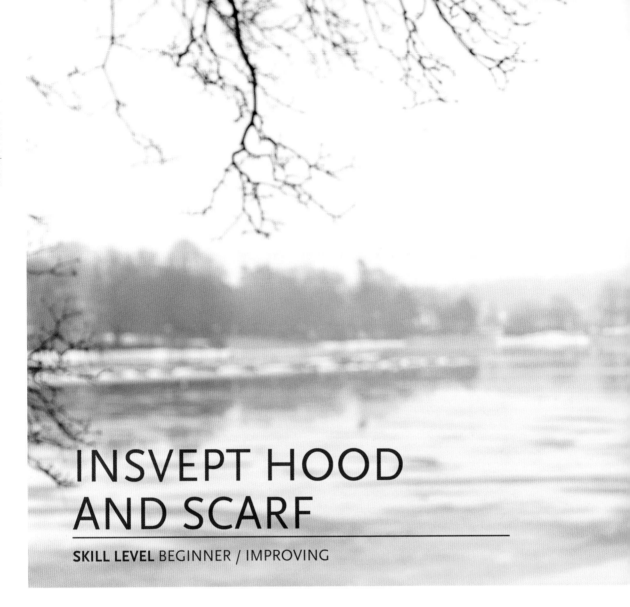

INSVEPT HOOD AND SCARF

SKILL LEVEL BEGINNER / IMPROVING

SIZES
To fit one size.

MATERIALS
Fourteen 50g/1¾oz balls of MillaMia Naturally Soft Merino in Putty Grey (121).
Pair of 5mm (US 8) knitting needles.

TENSION / GAUGE
18 sts and 30 rows to 10cm/4in square over moss st using 5mm (US 8) needles and yarn used double.

HINTS AND TIPS
Using the yarn double makes this scarf and hood nice and solid and warm. A simple construction, you can always adjust the length of the scarf to your own requirements.

ABBREVIATIONS
See page 11.

ALTERNATIVE COLOURWAYS

Storm	Seaside	Fawn	Berry	Petal
102	161	160	163	122

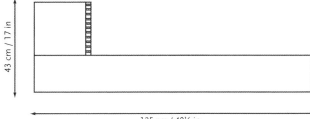

43 cm / 17 in

125 cm / 49¼ in

NOTE
Use yarn double **throughout.** This simply means using two balls of yarn at once. Using doubled yarn on a thicker needle (in our patterns a 5mm (US 8) needle) produces a thicker quality to the knitted fabric. An advantage of this technique is that the garment will be quicker to knit up.

SCARF (Make 2 pieces)
With 5mm (US 8) needles and yarn used double, cast on 31 sts.
Moss st row P1, [k1, p1] to end.
Cont in moss st until work measures 140cm/55in from cast on edge.
Cast off.

HOOD
With 5mm (US 8) needles and yarn used double, cast on 96 sts.
1st row (right side) P3, [k2, p2] to last 5 sts, k2, p3.
2nd row K3, [p2, k2] to last 5 sts, p2, k3.
Rep the last 2 rows twice more.
Cont in g-st until hood measures 27cm/10½in from cast on edge.
Cast off.

TO MAKE UP
Join last 27cm/10½in of each scarf piece to row ends of hood piece.
Fold hood in half and join back seam.

TEXTURED SIMPLICITY

A SIMPLE CONSTRUCTION MADE INTERESTING AND STRUCTURED
BY USING THE YARN DOUBLE.

SWISS DARNING

A number of the patterns in this book use a technique called Swiss darning (also sometimes known as 'duplicate stitch') that we feel is a great way to add little bits of colourwork to a design in a very effective way. It is also a technique that is a helpful alternative if you feel that you cannot do colourwork, or where only a small amount is required on a pattern. It represents an easier way to add small sections of colour after you complete an item. It can also be used to conceal mistakes.

With Swiss darning what you are doing is creating a second layer on top of the knitted fabric. You follow the pattern that is to be created using a separate piece of yarn and an embroidery needle (a needle with a rounded end is best so that it slips in and out of the stitches easily and does not split the yarn).

1 Bring the needle from the back of the knitted piece (the wrong side) to the front (the right side) through the base of the stitch to be covered. Then insert the needle from right to left behind the stitch directly above.

2 Insert the needle from front to back into the base of the stitch to be covered, then bring the needle through to the front again at the base of the next stitch to be covered. Do not pull the yarn too tight. The key is to have it too loose rather than too tight for even coverage. Try to keep the stitch the same size (tension) as the surrounding stitches.

3 Repeat the previous steps for all the stitches you wish the duplicate. You can do this in a straight line – horizontal or vertical – or in a pattern. If the yarn must skip a few stitches, bring the yarn past the stitches on the wrong side of the piece to keep the front side neat.

Finish off the Swiss darning. After completing the embellishment, secure the stitches before trimming the excess yarn. Either weave the end into the piece or tie the yarn to the base of the last stitch on the wrong side of the piece and trim it closely.

You can also look online on the MillaMia blog or other websites for further helpful tutorials and videos on this technique.

YARN COLOURS

Pitch Black 100

Midnight 101

Storm 102

Moss 103

Claret 104

Sable 105

Forget me not 120

Putty Grey 121

Petal 122

Lilac Blossom 123

Snow 124

Scarlet 140

Grass 141

Daisy Yellow 142

Fuchsia 143

Peacock 144

Fawn 160

Seaside 161

Plum 162

Berry 163

ABOUT MILLAMIA

MILLAMIA Established in late 2009 by two Swedish sisters, Katarina and Helena, MillaMia has quickly become recognised for its distinctive, modern knitting pattern designs and high quality yarn. Behind MillaMia is the belief that it should be possible to combine a love of knitting with a love of modern design and quality, with patterns influenced by the latest fashion trends, colours that work for every season and machine-washable wool made from the finest quality Merino wool. MillaMia is currently available throughout the UK and also internationally, including Australia, New Zealand, Sweden, Slovenia, Netherlands, Canada and the USA.

FROM MILLAMIA

It has been such an interesting experience for us taking the leap from managing the production of our books in-house to working with a publishing house. We hope you all enjoy the results – we are thrilled to produce a book of this scale, quality and breadth.

You will notice the important role of colour in our designs. When we defined the MillaMia Naturally Soft Merino colours we worked really hard to arrive at a set of shades that we felt would work well together, complementing and enhancing each other. As such, make sure you also have fun experimenting with different colour combinations. While we present options and alternative colour suggestions, why not try personalising your knitting by selecting your own variation of these? At www.millamia.com, you will find a 'Colour Tool' that allows you to experiment, 'playing' with different combinations and making your own colour design decisions.

We are always delighted to hear from people who have knitted or are thinking of knitting our items. Please do get in touch – let us know what you like, what you want to see next, what you would change – all feedback is welcome. And do let us know if you like the gingerbread!

Best wishes
Katarina and Helena
info@millamia.com

THANK YOUS

Thanks to our models
Adam, Alice, Amelia, Asa, Cornelia, Ferdinand, Fredrik, Helena, Isabel, Kristina, Mathilde, Mikael, Nohlia, Roshan, Sebastian, Selma, Stella.

Thanks to our knitters
Chris Davis, Sally Rogers, Sarah Ford, Geraldine Trower, Mhairi Sinclair.

Special thanks
To Asa for lending us her amazing home in Stockholm for this shoot and helping us source such incredible models, to Maja and Max for all their help in the run up to and preparation for the shoot, to Yumiko and Tanya for their ideas, enthusiasm and swatching and charting support, to our parents for their hoarding mentalilty which meant we had plenty of props to choose from, to Caroline who stopped by and helped with the kids as always, and to all the parents.

Credits
Design Helena Rosén
Design assistants Yumiko Isa and Tanya Leskinen
Pattern writing Penny Hill
Pattern checking Marilyn Wilson
Writing Katarina Rosén
Photography Emma Norén
Styling Lisa Harradine
Make up and hair Johanna Persson

Publishers' thanks
With thanks to Michelle Pickering for her excellent attention to detail and to Lisa Tai for her work on the layout.

PLAINFIELD PUBLIC LIBRARY
15025 S. Illinois Street
Plainfield, IL 60544